The
Farming
Game

Bryan Jones

The Farming Game

University of Nebraska Press, Lincoln & London

*Portions of this book have appeared in slightly
different form in the following publications
and are used with permission: "The Irrational
World of Farm Finance" in the* New Farm
*magazine, January 1981, pp. 34–39; "Sherman the
Scalper" in the* New Land Review, *no. 14,
1979–80.*

*Library of Congress Cataloging in Publication Data
Jones, Bryan, 1945–
The farming game.*

*1. Agriculture—High Plains (U.S.) 2. Farmers—
High Plains (U.S.) I. Title
S441.J68   1983   338.1'0978   82–2842
ISBN 0–8032–2559–8   AACR2*
THIRD PRINTING

To Butch, my best friend

Drawings by David Routon

Contents

Introduction

No one seemed to know why the government was suddenly interested in helping small farmers after spending the better part of thirty years systematically eliminating the species. But there we were, assembled in Des Moines, surrounded by bureaucrats from half a dozen government agencies and private think tanks. We had been divided into discussion groups and assigned various topics. From our testimony might come some lucrative program proposals to justify a new assault on the national treasury. While the tape recorders spun and the pinstripe set took notes, farmers dutifully went to work. They complained about interest rates, the government, low commodity prices, the government, inflation, the government, taxes, the government, inadequate access to capital, the government, a lack of leisure time, but mainly the government. None of the seasoned bureaucrats experienced any visible discomfort from the onslaught. Secure in their jobs, they took reams of notes and smiled pleasantly.

At one point during the controlled chaos, our oily little "facilitator," who moonlighted as a state Farmers Home administrator when he wasn't managing presidential campaigns, asked us to summarize our long-term farming goals. One wanted a bigger power boat. Another hoped that his grandchildren could inherit land that hadn't eroded into infertility. An organic farmer saw himself as a prophet spreading light through his own example. During the unusual period of quiet that followed while others pondered the question, I ventured that I wanted to make money and felt farming offered more attractive opportunities to accumulate large sums of capital than most other lines of endeavor. Those farmers that didn't boo did some serious hissing.

They informed me that it was impossible for farmers to make money. Sentiments like mine were dangerous to agriculture. Greed led fast-buck operators to wreak havoc on the land by overcropping and selling to foreign investors. I was expressing an unworthy motive before government bureaucrats who were there to help us and who would probably feel less charitable if we revealed ourselves to be as interested in filthy lucre as everyone else. One fellow farmer thought money might be suitable as a means to an end (farming the "right way") but not as an end in itself. With that, we moved to more important questions concerning the general incompetency of Farmers Home administrators and the need for parity pricing of farm commodities. We completed our work, and the record of deliberation is presumably filed in a government computer somewhere. The original impetus for the conference died a quick death. Perhaps government funding had run short of expectations or some new oppressed minority had stolen our limelight. At any rate, small-farm problems were put on a back burner.

In the months since, I have listened more closely when farmers discuss their aspirations. The unifying theme of these conversations is concern for money in all its various forms. Most of my acquaintances want more of that commodity than they now have. The precise method of gaining the objective is usually the subject under discussion. How can anyone afford to buy land at these prices? Should I plant more soybeans this year, or will the Brazilians flood the market? What are bred cows selling for, and can I expect a profit if I buy some?

Were the delegates in Des Moines a subspecies with completely different characteristics? Were they lying to themselves? Don't power boats and more leisure time imply an increase in income? Does a greed deficiency hamper small farmers in their survival efforts? These questions begot more. What personal qualities allow some farmers to prosper compared to others? Where is the farming industry headed? How did we get where we are? Is federal agricultural policy shortsighted or part of some rational master plan? Would an increase in the farm population result in national social benefits? Could a model farming operation be constructed that could be followed by rookies?

The Farming Game is the result of my curiosity. Most of the agricultural activities I am describing are located on the High Plains area of Kansas, Nebraska, Oklahoma, North Texas, eastern Colorado, and the Dakotas. This was the last region of the country to be settled, and in many ways it remains a land of opportunity. Land is not as expensive as elsewhere in the country. There are few restrictions on economic mobility, and society is relatively open. The High Plains area has never matured socially; changes have come too rapidly. Farm communities were barely established when the Great Depression tore families from the land and scattered them to the winds. High prices and adequate rainfall during World War II helped the survivors to gain a tentative financial stability that lasted until 1953. Then Ezra Taft Benson, Eisenhower's secretary of agriculture, launched his massive program of forced urbanization that has been continued somewhat haphazardly by his disciples to the present day.

Growing conditions on the High Plains could best be described as erratic. Devastating hailstorms and intense periods of drought are common enough to make two good crop years in a row a cause for general rejoicing. A farmer in Illinois may cry about a dry spell two weeks old, whereas a Kansas farmer might feel fortunate to get three good rains during a whole summer. This explains in part why land in this area is relatively inexpensive compared with land in states where crop yields are more predictable. The constant threat of financial ruin loosens folks up and is a definite social leveler. Who is going to put his nose in the air when next week's hailstorm could wipe him out? A family whose wealth is in deep, black Illinois farmland with forty inches of annual rainfall can count on some sort of an income. They might plan ten years ahead of time to send a daughter to an expensive finishing school. After the pocket calculator hits a half million or so, they may move up to a better country club and trade the old Buick on a Mercedes. A farmer on the High Plains might come up with the same total and see half of it evaporate in one summer of blistering drought. This is not to say that plains society is totally egalitarian, far from it. It is just that the social vibrations emanating from Washington, Kansas, are considerably more relaxed than those of Quincy, Illinois, where land is held in firm hands and changes ownership only once every two centuries or so. It is a rare country newspaper on the High Plains that hasn't a couple of sale bills printed inside, and during tough times there may be a dozen a week. Ownership is difficult to obtain if no one wants to sell. Since capital accumulation in general and land acquisition in particular are the goals of the game, an area where land is sold regularly has an advantage for the novice and experienced player alike. That is why the rougher, drier parts of the High Plains offer perhaps the best chance for the small farmer to survive and the best opportunity for new people to enter the business.

This is the area where I live and farm. My wife and I began a small cattle operation in 1972 while working at other jobs. At present, we have a diversified grain and livestock operation featuring dairy and beef cattle, sheep, hogs, and even a few Angora goats. Farm life has been a rich experience, especially because of the many fascinating people we have met. Certainly, without the personal foibles of the farmers who appear as Shaky Ed, Crazy Billy, and Ike Grable, this book would not have been nearly so much fun to write.

*Well, there's farmers, and then
there's the rest of the population.*

B. J. Tupper

The Last Capitalist

"We sold fat cattle last week, lost a hundred dollars a head."

My college professor friend was appalled. "How are you going to survive that kind of loss?"

"It wasn't so bad, a lot of the feedlot boys are losing a hundred and fifty per head, but we bought some cheap feeder cattle and it paid off. I think maybe this market has bottomed out and it might be a good time to lay in some feeder cattle. The price is bound to go up, it always does."

"But a hundred dollars a head is hard to make up, isn't it?"

"Yeah, it's tough, but as long as the banker doesn't get too nervous, we'll hang in there."

"What's to say the market can't go down even more? I know *we* don't eat steak as often as we used to, and neither do our friends. Wouldn't you be better off just farming? Why risk losing another ten or twenty thousand?"

"I guess I could just farm. Even though there are plenty of risks there, too, it probably would be the smart thing to do. I could really cut down on my borrowing, and there would be less work and worry."

"Why don't you do it then?"

"Because it wouldn't be nearly so exciting."

"Exciting? What's so exciting about losing money? It sounds positively boring to me."

"It's hard to explain. A man gets a hundred thousand dollars wrapped up in a project that he might lose his shirt on, and that can get exciting. So is buying the feeder cattle in the first place. Cattle auctions are competitive. One man is always trying to buy cheaper than another and there isn't much time to decide. That's exciting. There's the time when the cattle are getting fat and sleek and, to my notion, beautiful. That's exciting. Then there's the selling end. A roily boily market can make the marketing decisions absolutely vital. Make a mistake and you could drop some serious money. Guess right and you could maybe have enough money to pay on last year's loss. I think even you'd agree that's mildly interesting."

"Does everyone that feeds cattle do it for kicks?"

"No, actually most of them do it as a business. It's the commercial feedlots that feed most of our fat cattle these days. They don't care what the price is because they get their money regardless. The man that feeds on his own doesn't account for much of the market anymore. Those that are still in the racket have to be in it for the excitement because there hasn't been any profit for a long time."

"I don't understand."

"It's hard to explain."

My friend had fallen victim to the popular misconception that American agriculture is operated on an easily understood, rational basis.

TV news commentators continually spout platitudes like "Since the price of pork is up 10 percent this month, farmers will increase production to meet the demand, and prices should come down next fall"; or, "Because farmers in Kansas suffered 100 percent hail loss last night, you can expect the price of wheat to go up, and *that* will be reflected in the supermarket in the coming months."

Such statements of cause and effect are far too simple. Will a hailstorm in Kansas push up the price of bread? It may or it may not, depending on what the government and the bakers do. Let's say Pleezesqueeze Super Bread sells for ninety-five cents a loaf. About three cents worth of wheat is used in making each loaf. If the entire wheat crop of Kansas is hailed out and wheat jumps a dollar a bushel, it might increase Pleezesqueeze's costs one cent a loaf. Pleezesqueeze could increase its price to ninety-six cents, unless the Saveabuck Grocery chain decides to market its economy loaf at the old price and absorb the cost increase in favor of greater volume. For greater volume, Pleezesqueeze may also be willing to absorb that penny. Or both may shrink their loaves a fraction, or beat more air into the dough, or increase the proportion of nonwheat ingredients, or do a couple of other things that might save a penny. On the other hand, if Pleezesqueeze and Saveabuck think a price rise is in order, they may say that the high wheat costs brought on by the Kansas hailstorm has caused them to raise prices four cents a loaf.

If the hailstorm in Kansas has wiped out a big chunk of the nation's wheat crop, the price of wheat will initially rise. The Department of Agriculture might then step in, dumping some of its stocks on the market, dropping its loan rate to farmers, or embargoing grain sales to some large communist country. Any of these actions will depress prices and help quiet consumers. Pleezesqueeze might use the hailstorm as an excuse to raise its bread price four cents a loaf when in reality government manipulation has dropped wheat costs down to two and a half cents per loaf. Wheat farmers will froth at the mouth, rail at government interference with the marketplace, and plant a 20 percent larger wheat crop the next chance they get.

Perhaps we should be sympathetic to the network news producer who must educate the public about the intricacies of agriculture in one thirty-second spot every month or so. Farmers do not always behave rationally, and certainly markets do not behave rationally, as thousands of rueful commodity players will tell you. American agriculture cannot be described in simple terms. Nonetheless, the national media with their chronic affection for good guy–bad guy news continue to treat farmers as if they were retarded children to be pitied (in the case of natural disaster) or scorned (in the case of high beef prices). It should not be surprising that nonfarmers have a general ignorance of America's largest industry.

The truth is that farmers occupy the most privileged class in America. They enjoy the greatest opportunity for real wealth and the nearest thing to personal freedom that exists in this country.

Socially, farmers have enormous personal latitude. No self-respecting farmer gives a damn whether his neighbor went to school at NYU or MIT, as long as he doesn't use ten-dollar words or sneer at the natives. On the other hand, an NYU graduate could use ten-dollar words, wear purple silk underwear, and sneer at the natives, and it might not hinder his economic progress one iota. A graduate at Fort Hays State who wears cowboy boots probably won't be in line for a major promotion at Chase Manhattan, which might explain why eastern banks make all those weird loans to little countries and don't pay much in the way of dividends. A man who makes $150,000 a year and is worth a couple of million dollars, who favors twenty-four-dollar Key overalls, wears various types of barnyard substances on his shoes, whose pickup-truck cab looks like a junkie's nightmare, and whose haircut looks like a 1944 Auschwitz model might be allowed to live in Winnetka, but it's doubtful his neighbors would embrace him socially. In the world of farming, one needs only to be friendly, unpretentious, and honest to gain the neighborhood's acceptance. Some are hostile, pretentious, and crooked and don't fare too badly either.

This is not to say that there are no classes of farmers; quite the contrary. Some have planes and spend the winters in Vail or Tucson; others milk goats and drive '48 Fords. But the common bonds of dealing with weather, the government, and farm implements tend to keep relationships on a human level. A big operator may covet the land of a small farmer and may even wage economic war to obtain what he wants. He may sneer at the inefficiencies of the operation in question, but he usually retains a grudging respect for his intended victim. Compare this with situations where whole city neighborhoods have been dissolved by urban renewal, where union members strike against employers they have never seen, or where employers lay off workers whose names are known permanently only to their computers. Agriculture remains a personal business in an impersonal society.

On comparison with the rest of the working public it will be generally true that farmers have a much more varied work load and experience fewer of the grinding day-to-day frustrations with their fellow man. Farmers have plenty of frustrations, but they are likely to be different ones each day. Some farmers work like crazy in the spring. Some work like crazy in the fall. A few work moderately hard all the time. But few experience exactly the same routine every day. There are trips to town for parts and money, breakdowns, sometimes a sow to farrow, sometimes a day to load and sell cattle. Sometimes it rains, and they can do very little. Always there's a good chance a neighbor may drop by for a chat, and now and then a salesman arrives to be shooed away, or humored, as the case may be. Farmers have a flexible schedule and no boss but themselves.

With all their personal freedom, farmers may be the most financially exploited class in the nation. Governments kowtow to consumers by holding down farm prices, local governments tax farmland at ruinous rates, and eastern elitists are continually conspiring to drive a few hundred thousand people from the farm to cheapen up the labor market. Nonetheless, the sheer size of the parasitic industries that farmers support (farm equipment, banking, chemical, fertilizer, land-grant universities, and transportation) attests to the tremendous wealth generated by farmers every year.

Agriculture produces new wealth constantly from renewable resources. The sun's energy is transformed into corn, wheat, alfalfa, cotton, and ultimately into pork, beef, mutton, and clothing. Ewes have lambs, and lambs grow into ewes and have other lambs. Each new lamb and each new bushel of wheat is new wealth with real worth. The renewable nature of agriculture is the basic reason why farmers can become wealthy so easily, compared to people in other pursuits.

Joe Johnson, steelworker, may make $25,000 per year between lay-offs. If his wife is a good manager, and if Joe has few expensive habits, he could be expected to make a car payment on a vehicle that will depreciate in value every day he owns it, make payments on a house that will appreciate at approximately twice the rate of inflation, and perhaps sock $2,500 per year into the money market where he could draw as much as 18 percent. Joe will never get ahead on his car investment because it will wear out and he will need to buy another, probably at a much higher price. Repairs will be a constant drain on his resources. The car will eat oil, gas, tires, and insurance payments, not to speak of interest at a substantial rate. By no stretch of the imagination can Joe's car be regarded as a part of Joe's capital. Cars should always be entered on the liability side of the ledger. Joe's house is quite another matter. If he sold the house, he could probably recover the taxes and interest he had paid over the years and have some left over to pay the real estate agent's commission. Joe needs a place to live, that much is clear. However, his biggest investment in most cases produces no net income. Joe's savings represent his real accumulated capital. His accumulated capital yields him 15 percent interest. With some real luck and restraint on the part of the Arabs he may come out even vis-à-vis inflation, which is more than can be said for his house and his car. Our mythical Joe may also have some life insurance, but the interest rate on that is laughable, and since he can only beat the system by dying young in an accident (an event of dubious worth to himself), we shall leave a discussion of the merits of life insurance to the folks who sell it.

Consider Joe's assets invested in agriculture. At today's prices Joe could purchase eight bred gilts, a boar, and their feed for one year with his $2,500 savings. If he were to succeed at farrowing at an average rate, he would sell 112 pigs at $40, or $4,448. That's about 170 percent interest. Chances are that Joe's feed, depreciation, and investment tax credits would completely cover his tax liability. Obviously, things are not all that simple. Joe must know something about hogs, the hogs must stay healthy, the neighbors need to be understanding. But the possibility exists nonetheless. Let's say Joe's house sits upon one and one-half acres of usable ground. If one acre of his crabgrass-free, turf-built lawn were plowed up and sown to wheat, Joe would have invested approximately $15, not counting his land cost, which he had anyway because he has to live someplace. If it rains, doesn't hail, and Joe can get the kids to do a decent job of threshing on the garage floor, he should end up with about forty bushels of wheat at about $4.50 per bushel, or $180 minus his original $15, or 1,100 percent interest in new wealth. It may even beat the rate of inflation.

These two examples are, of course, simplified. They are used to show how new capital can be generated quickly in agriculture. Later we will look at a more realistic picture of how this works in practice. The important thing to remember is that agriculture is a ready source of new, real capital and that it is renewable, unlike most other forms of wealth.

If farming is so rewarding, why aren't folks flocking to the countryside? Aside from the fact that the true nature of farming has been such a well-kept secret, the reason is that farms are too expensive for most of them to buy. People seldom enter agriculture as a career unless they inherit a farm. This unfortunate circumstance was brought about by deliberate government policy and by the capital-intensive evolution of modern agriculture.

President Eisenhower's secretary of agriculture, Ezra Taft Benson, pushed a soil bank law through Congress which, coupled with Eisenhower's interstate highway plan, completely altered American society. Benson's soil bank scheme was intended to reduce agricultural production and funnel the resulting surplus of farm workers into the urban job market. Production was not controlled significantly because only the most marginal farmland was put into this land-retirement program. In the South particularly, large chunks of worn-out tenant farms were stuck in the soil bank for ten years in return for small yearly payments. Huge numbers of former tenants, largely black, were forced into the core areas of northern cities. In the Great Plains, another area with a large concentration of marginal land, small rural villages that had survived the dirty thirties wasted away overnight as tenant farmers left their rented land for the job market of urban America.* Most midwestern white ex-farmers found a ready market for their mechanical abilities and began earning more cash money than they'd ever seen in their lives. The black farmers met with less success due to discrimination and some lack of mechanical job skills. However, with the increasing automation of the late fifties and sixties, unskilled jobs disappeared from the job market rapidly. Factories began to move out of the urban core areas. Meanwhile, Eisenhower's interstate highway program,

*In the single year of 1956, one out of every eleven rural people moved to the city.

which was originally budgeted for $33 billion, enabled cities to construct new freeways, making the ensuing flight to the suburbs that much easier. Whole populations of central city neighborhoods disappeared, to reappear dispersed on Long Island or in Arlington Heights. Work in the city and sleep in the suburbs would likely have become common without Eisenhower's program. However, a city lacking an extensive freeway structure, such as New Orleans until the late 1960s, might have found itself renovating and preserving its core areas rather than allowing them to become blighted and replaced by high-rise, low-income monstrosities. Thus the Benson and Eisenhower obsession with cheap labor and adequate transportation combined to destroy the health of rural communities and the life of the core areas of many of our major cities as well. Had the Agriculture Department spent the $1.2 billion it spent on the soil bank on a serious attempt to finance farm purchases for rural blacks, and had it spent some effort on developing marketing co-ops for small farm production, our social history of the past twenty years might have been very different.

With the active help of Ezra Taft Benson, Orville Freeman, Earl Butz, Bob Bergland, and, most recently, John Block, American agriculture has developed into a capital-intensive business. Land-grant universities have also pursued lines of research that have benefited large commercial operations, to the detriment of small farmers and rural communities. Farm policies adopted by commercial banks, the Farmers Home Administration, Production Credit associations, large insurance companies, and the Federal Land Bank have put additional premiums on increased size and large capital expenditures in farm operations.

The term *capital-intensive* essentially means replacing labor with machinery. It can mean that a dairy farmer moves from milking cows by hand (which effectively limits the size of his herd to the amount of labor available) to an automated pipeline milking machine (which limits the size of his herd to the number of cows he can afford to feed and house). It can mean buying a $100,000 four-wheel-drive tractor so that one man can farm his land in less time than he did before. Where adequate groundwater is available, he may spend $70,000 to install a center-pivot irrigation system on some of his marginal land, thereby increasing both his repayment liabilities and his cash flow. He will more than likely use expensive herbicides and insecticides on his own crops rather than weed the crops or engage in crop rotation practices that would limit the size of his operation by increasing the man hours of labor required. He may choose to purchase a $100,000 hog-finishing operation rather than continue to deal with the problems of heat and cold, hauling bedding, and the constant job of fixing fence and chasing wayward piggies. He will rely on sulfas, penicillin, virginiamycin, Mecadox, or other drugs to control his disease problems rather than move his hogs to clean ground every year or so. He may purchase an expensive piece of land so that he can impress his lender with a steady asset growth curve and ensure an increasing supply of capital.

Most agricultural lenders encourage these practices, including the government's own Farmers Home Administration. The official position is that since farms are bound to get larger, they're going to bet their lending funds on those farmers who will be among the survivors of consolidation. Show them a machinery inventory that does not include a fifty-thousand-dollar combine, a fifteen-thousand-dollar truck, or at least a couple of thirty-thousand-dollar tractors and their eyeballs begin to glaze over. Show them a cash flow that includes no cash grain sales and they check their watches every two minutes. Talk about improving the soil by plowing down clover instead of raising corn and they will have to be somewhere five minutes ago. After all, it takes no longer to write a million dollar loan than it does one of ten thousand.

For the past twenty-five years the Department of Agriculture has pursued policies that put a premium on large production units. In periods when the government has made price-support payments, extremely high limits have been placed on payments to individual farmers. At the present time this limit is $50,000. In the state of Nebraska, 46 percent of the farmers do not even *gross* $50,000 per year. Had crop-deficiency payments been raised (the difference between the set target price and the present market price) and total payments to individual producers lowered to a reasonable level, say $8,000, the end result would have been the stabilization of small-farm numbers. Crop loans and the companion storage payments have always benefited larger producers that carry a lower per-unit cost and have been able to justify the erection of large storage structures (on money loaned by the government at a favorable rate).

Each year the average American farm size increases, and each year a decreasing number of farmers receive a larger share of government payments. Average farm indebtedness rises every year as increasing amounts of technology are injected into the production cycle. Farming has become a very big business indeed. Our task here is not to applaud this turn of events, nor to instruct the reader in the mysteries of 200-bushel corn production or the use of Ramrod Atrazine. This type of production is out of reach for the vast majority of potential farmers anyway. By reviewing the operations of some typical farmer capitalists, we may begin to see some viable alternatives to taking a half million dollars and buying ourselves a full-time job that pays seven thousand dollars a year.

Real
Farmers

*The dumbest farmer always
raises the biggest beets.*

Old Swedish Saying

Shaky Ed: Neatness as a Virtue

Shaky Ed grows a great deal of corn in our part of the world. Last year he raised 174,000 bushels of the stuff. Occasionally Ed makes a profit on his crop, which is fortunate because his recent land purchases require large interest and principle payments. The pressure of needing maximum production every year causes Shaky Ed to lose his sanity during the critical planting period each spring, which is how he earned his nickname.

He believes corn is a fragile vegetable species subject to a host of enemies, all of which by association become Ed's enemies. Just as a dirty tractor or an unpainted building disgusts Ed, excessively wet or dry planting conditions that may cause herbicide failure and attendant high weed population drive him to distraction.

"Weeds are always waitin' around for a guy to screw up on his herbicide, then they sneak out and grow like hell. I can't stand weeds. They make a farm look bad. Sure, a man can cultivate 'em out of the middle of the row, but you can't git 'em out of the ridge. Anybody drives by, they think I'm a lousy farmer."

New corn diseases threaten periodically, forcing Ed to scour the countryside for resistant varieties. Usually he beats his neighbors to the punch and has all the available resistant seed locked up before planting time. Most corn diseases spoil the appearance of the plant, giving it a sickly color or stunting its growth. However, Ed does not hate corn disease nearly to the extent that he hates insects. Cutworms, corn borer, ear worms, spider mites, and rootworms march through Ed's brain almost every summer night as he tries to sleep. Sometimes he has nightmares in January. These fears have made Ed slightly paranoid on the subject of bugs. He imparts humanlike motives to insects, as in "Those spider mites are trying to bankrupt me," or "You have to watch rootworms or they'll lay in the ground, wait for the bug dope to break down, and then out they'll come and chew the hell out of things." Occasionally he will attribute insect infestations to the hidden workings of the Trilateral Commission who, as everyone knows, spend most of its waking hours scheming to effect bankruptcy on little farmers like Ed. "They want us broke so we have to keep growing big crops every year to stay in business. What better way to keep us broke than churn out new bugs all the time? They've probably got a laboratory in Russia that makes hybrid rootworms on a full-time basis, and just as soon as we get a bug dope that'll work, they have their stooges in the EPA shut it off."

Where most farmers strive for high yields and attendant coffee shop bragging rights, Ed works toward a totally sterile crop environment. The only good bug is a dead bug. "Usually I kill most of 'em by using preplant insecticides and aerial spraying early in the hatch. Most guys wait till the bugs are on the dessert course before they call in the flyboys. If I see a corn borer moth, I git to a phone pronto."

I see Ed frequently in the coffee shop where he holds winter lectures on government, social issues, and farm economics. Ed converted from the Farm Bureau to the American Agriculture Movement several years ago, and while his philosophy contains elements absorbed from those esteemed organizations, his outlook can only be described as unique. I have to own up to occasionally baiting Ed. Usually he kicks the furniture and swears, which is a whole lot more fun than the time or two when he became violent.

"You make any money raising corn this year, Ed?"

"Make money? Are you kiddin'? We're gittin' the sale bills printed up next week."

"What do you figure on doing next year? These hog boys might make some real money."

"Ya, sure, an' they might not. I'll be damned if I'll have them stinkin' sonsabitches eatin' up all my buildings an' fence. Sure as I'd git in 'em, the price'd bust all to hell an' then where would I be? Dad had some hogs once an' it took us two years just to get rid of the stink. Always gittin' out, rootin' up the yard—who needs 'em?"

"I hear these cattle boys might be smelling clover this year. You've got enough corn to feed some out."

"Well, I wouldn't mind feedin' a few calves, but I ain't set up for it, an' by the time you figger yer labor, you ain't got nothin' left anyhow. The calf market is crazy and them boys that's buyin' are goin' to git burnt sure as hell. Besides, cattle stink almost as bad as hogs an' are always rubbin' fences down."

"If you're so set on raising corn, why don't you take a look at Tony's operation? He claims going organic has saved him 50 percent on production costs."

"Good Lord, Jones, you don't believe that crap do you? The state university boys say it ain't worth a damn, an' I know it ain't worth a damn. One year I used some bug killer at the recommended level, and I bet I didn't kill half of 'em. Now I always go three times the dosage. Fry 'em, that's what I say. Where would I be, doin' like old Organic Tony? Bugs runnin' out my ears, that's where. I ain't even talkin' about no fertilizer or no herbicide or no yield, for Chrissake! I suppose you're one of them crazy environmentalists that wants us to hoe our crops in the hot sun till our young asses drop off, huh? You saw ol' Organic Tony out there all summer with that washed out little wife of his an' his little snot-nosed kids scratchin' around in that godforsaken patch of PINTO BEANS! Me, I was driving around in an air-conditioned GMC pickup truck watchin' the corn grow while they was sweatin' like pigs. You want me to do that?"

"Well, they did get $18 a bushel for their beans, and Tony says he didn't borrow much operating money this year."

"Ya, well maybe he did an' then maybe he didn't. He probably raised a hell of a lot more bugs to infest the neighborhood than he did beans. You know who my hero is, Jones? That Darth Vader from *Star Wars*. Everytime I cook up a little Roundup or Atrazine, I think about all the weeds I'm going to fry. An' every time I buy a couple of tons of Furadan, I think about all the rootworms I'm going to seriously incinerate. My flyboys get a coupla hundred birds a year when they lay on the Parathion. Damned birds crap on everything they don't eat. You give me the right stuff an' I could kill every damned bird an' bug on my farm."

"Tony says farmers get cancer more often than they used to. He claims it's these chemicals everybody uses."

"Tony said that, did he? That figures. He always was chicken. Hell, if he'd use an outfit like mine, he wouldn't have any worries."

"What outfit is that?"

"I like to call it my Darth Vader outfit. You know, rubber gloves, face mask, the whole bit. I put it on when I'm mixin' the stuff to kill the bugs. I wouldn't let ol' Tony worry me none if I was you, Jones. Guys like him won't last long anyhow. What's he got, eighty acres? There ain't a building on it that's got a decent coat of paint. Isn't any banker going to loan a guy money that don't paint his stuff or kill his bugs. Screws up the neighborhood for the rest of us, if nothin' else."

"I'm a little confused, Ed. If you aren't making any money growing corn, what are you going to raise next year?"

"I guess maybe I'll plant just the same as always and hope the price goes up. Hell, it can't stay down where it's at, nobody will raise the stuff, and then where will the damned government git its cheap grain?"

I found Ed's logic irresistible. If everybody like Ed planted as usual, where indeed would the government get its cheap grain?

"Do you figure we're going to get any help on grain prices?"

"Not really. The government will probably jack up the loan rate on corn a dime or two. That'll put me in the black at least. I still will be losin' money on my investment, of course, but what the hell? I'll probably put up a couple a bins and wait for the Chinks to starve some year. You wait, them damned New York Jews will git tired of losing money in the stock market.* Then you watch the corn and soybeans smoke. All of a sudden you'll hear all kinds of rumors about Brazil not havin' no soybeans and Australia burning up with drought. Last year every damned cobra jockey in India could have croaked and nobody would have heard a word. That's 'cause them Jew boys had all sold short. They own all the damned newspapers and TV stations, you know. This year they'll all go long, you wait an' see. We're going to have famine news runnin' out of our ears."

Most winters in recent years Ed has found time to go to Washington to lobby for higher grain prices. I asked him if he'd had a good time this year. He said it wasn't any wonder how come Wilber Mills and that Hays fella had got in so much

---

*There are those in the financial community who feel that the Gnomes of Zurich control the financial destiny of the world through all sorts of unfathomable manipulation. For some farmers, the Gnomes of Zurich are replaced by the New York Jewish community, which is credited with everything from selling the country out to the Russians to knocking fifty cents off the price of hogs in Peoria on any given day.

trouble with all those loose women runnin' around. They had talked to a lot of eastern congressmen, pleading their case for higher prices. Ed was surprised that other parts of the country had some good representatives. "Hell, before I went down there I figgered they'd all be a bunch of pinko-commies, the way they vote on welfare and farm bills, but most of 'em ain't half bad. Some of 'em got brains. Maybe only 10 to 20 percent are reds, or else maybe they hide it real good. It was hard to get some of them to listen to how bad off we are. You'd think they'd have a little more concern for the future of their god-damned country. Hell, I could buy and sell most of them politicians, an' they got nerve enough to tell me they're concerned with the high cost of food, as if farm prices had anything to do with it."

I stopped by Ed's farm the other day to see about getting some fertilizer applied. He was out in the machine shed waxing his tractor.

"Jesus, Ed, you think that'll make it run any better, shining it up like that?"

Ed gave the fender an extra swipe and grinned. "Well, maybe not, but she shore looks a hell of a lot better. You leave these babies unprotected and they get to lookin' crummy pretty fast. Ol' Grable down the road has had his over a year an' hasn't even washed it."

I said Grable never traded tractors anyway and had maybe bought the last one he'd ever buy.

"Well, he might die, ya know. Then they'll sell his stuff and it won't bring nothin' if she don't shine. Then where will his heirs be? Suckin' air, that's where. I know for a fact he hasn't put new tires on that A John Deere for twenty years. A guy can't do business like that an' git along."

I pointed out that Grable had done pretty well and probably didn't owe anyone in the world a red cent.

"Ya, but I'd like to see him try it nowadays with things as

tough as they are. Hell, I got to borrow money just to live on, for Chrissake. Grable don't even own a fertilizer applicator, hires me to do it. No rinky-dink operation like that could make it starting out without no fertilizer applicator." I winced a little and started moving toward the door. "Stick around. You can help me paint the granary."

I pointed out he had painted the granary six months ago, and if he put any more coats of paint on it, the weight would probably crush the foundation.

"Well, you got to keep things up. Once you let 'er go, you can't ever git 'er back to where she was. I'll bet Grable ain't painted his barn in forty years an' you can see what that man's place looks like. I don't see how he stays in business operating like that. No banker would look at him twice, I can tell you that."

I pointed out that Grable owned a good chunk of the local bank.

"Ya, but if he didn't he couldn't git no loan. Us guys that keep our places up got to pay more taxes than him too; it ain't fair."

I could see Shaky was upset (thinking about Grable always did that), and I wasn't about to ask him to put on fertilizer, so I headed for the pickup.

"What did you want to see me about anyway?"

"Oh, I thought maybe I could sell you some tractor wax, but I see you've got plenty."

"Ya, I do, but I'll catch you next time. I'm going to have to work on my combine pretty quick, it ain't lookin' so good."

The air conditioning works a lot better than the last one I had.

Big Feeling Fred

Big Machinery
– Big Feeler

Big feelers are experts on everything from international trade to the farming practices of their social inferiors. They are seldom shy about expressing their views and are never wrong. At least, they never remember being wrong. Some Big Feelers think they are important people by virtue of owning vast tracts of land. It is not unusual to hear them brag of being self-made men, even if the land was an outright gift from a senile uncle. Big Feelers can gain their lofty status by belonging to churches or organizations heavily populated by other Big Feelers. They can also become important persons by acquiring newer and larger machinery than their neighbors. Seldom is the machinery stored in a shed until it has spent sufficient time in the front yard to inform the entire community of the new purchase. Most often no real justification exists for the ownership of the new machine except the joy of owning.

Fred lives on a rented farm and leases the two center pivots installed on it. Last year Fred raised 260 acres of irrigated corn, which made 65 bushels to the acre. Fred also raised 50 acres of wheat, none of which was ever harvested because he didn't get to it. Although he's been a farmer for over thirty years, Fred has never bought any land. Therefore his entire net worth is tied up in machinery. The total farm production for last year was 14,950 bushels of corn, half of which belonged to the land-lord. Fred put his share in the elevator and took a government loan on it. After moisture docks, drying charges, and prepaid storage costs, he was paid $2.43 per bushel, or $18,164. His production costs were $46,800. On his crops alone Fred lost $28,636. However, by custom swathing 3,000 acres of hay at $4.50 an acre, baling 6,000 large round bales at $5.00 a bale, custom harvesting 800 acres of wheat at $8.00 an acre, and picking 500 acres of corn at 20 cents a bushel, Fred picked up an additional $61,900. The reason for the poor crop year was that Fred was so busy custom harvesting that he could never find time to turn on his sprinklers or cut his own wheat. He did find time to trade in some machinery, however. His old swather bought last year at $14,000 went in on a new one at $24,000 (the new one has a cab and air-conditioning); his old combine bought last year at $55,000 went in on a new one at $85,000; a round baler bought two years ago at $6,500 went in on a new one at $8,500; his pickup that had cost $8,400 in 1980 went in on a $11,500 job; and a truck that had set him back $12,000 in 1974 went in on a new twenty footer at $36,800. Fred had virtually no equity in any of the machines he traded off, with the exception of the pickup and truck, which he had financed through the bank. By trading with the machinery companies that had financed his equipment, Fred was able to add the new purchase price onto what he still owed on the old machine. Therefore, his new machinery, added to what he owed on the old machines, comes to a cool $154,000, which, added to a few discs, planters, cultivators, and odd equipment, brings his total machinery indebtedness to $225,000 at 18 percent interest. All the loans are set up on three years, so his annual payment this year will be $115,500. Fred also must pay his lease on the two pivots, which is set up on ten years at 12 percent or $14,520. Thus his total payments are $130,020 on a net income of $33,264, of which $14,000 had to come out for living expenses. This deficit of $96,756 might be covered if Fred had some land to borrow on. He doesn't. His machinery has declined in value rather than gone up, so each year his position will further deteriorate. Luckily Fred has a kindly uncle who invested the entire proceeds from the sale of his large farm in treasury notes. Thus, year after year Fred's deficits are made up by a cheerful benefactor who enjoys watching the sweat roll off his nephew's face every time he comes with a new tale of woe—which just goes to show you how access to free money can make a fool out of most anyone.

I stopped by Fred's place to see if he could find time to put on my fertilizer. He was busy parking his new tractor and baler in the front yard. Fred looked happy. I figured I'd come at a good time.

"It looks like the price of baling is about to go up again."

"No, actually I think I'll drop down to $4.50 a bale this year. It's only fair; this baby doesn't make bales as big as the other one did."

"Not as big? How come you got a baler that makes smaller bales? I don't know anything about baling, but that sounds a little strange to me."

"Ya, it does sound a little strange, but those other guys were making 800-pound bales and charging $4.00 a bale, and I was makin' 1,700-pound bales and chargin' $5.00, which is over twice as cheap, right?"

"Right."

"Wrong. They thought those other guys were cheaper because they only charged $4.00, and I lost a couple of jobs. Besides, everybody busted up their loaders trying to lift those big jobs and I got cussed out for it. This one will turn out 1,200-pound bales, and I'll explain to 'em how $4.50 for 1,200 pounds is cheaper than $4.00 for 800 pounds, and maybe we'll get along better."

"Couldn't your old baler make smaller bales if you set it differently?"

"Ya, but you had to keep setting the goddamned tension on

it, and it was unhandy as hell. Some guys, like old Grable, wanted them as big as I could get 'em, and other guys not so big. It'd take me half an hour just to change the damn thing, and then I wasn't sure it was right till I baled a couple. Besides that, this one doesn't have any belts. The old one had belts that always broke and it'd take a couple of hours just to fix 'em."

"I thought those belts didn't cost too much."

"They don't, compared to other repairs, but I don't have time to mess with 'em. When you've got hay down and it's time to bale, then you do it. Otherwise everyone's mad at you and next time they get somebody else, even if they don't do a good job."

"Nice tractor."

"I about had to trade, the other one was almost shot. The cab started leakin' dust."

"Couldn't you fill in with foam rubber?"

"Oh, I suppose, but these new cabs are twice as good, and it will bring a lot more when I go to trade it in."

"You're going to trade it in? I thought you just bought it."

"Oh, I think I'll wait till fall. You get a better trade-in then. In the spring everybody wants 'em. They've got a new one comin' out that's got a hydrostatic drive, kind of an automatic transmission, and it will work a lot better on the baler than this old one. We won't ever have to gear down in a heavy windrow, just pour the coals to her, and she'll do the rest."

"Old? You just bought this tractor for Chrissake!"

"They're always changin' 'em. If you don't keep up, you can't get nothing on a trade-in. You take Grable. His stuff is so old he'd make those dealers fall on the ground laughin' if he ever brought it in for a trade. He's still driving an A John Deere he bought new in 1948. I don't think he's ever put tires on it even. What would he get for it on a 1086—$600 if he was lucky? I don't know how he stays in business."

I pointed out that Grable owned one implement dealership outright and a half interest in another.

"Oh, he just owns them so he can get his parts cheap. If he didn't own them, you can bet those guys wouldn't truck with a rinky dink like that. He doesn't even own a fertilizer applicator. He was over here yesterday cryin' that Shaky Ed wouldn't do it for him right away, so I had to go do it. That guy's somethin' else."

I started moving for the pickup, but Fred kept on.

"That Ed's something else, too. You know he's got the same planter he bought eight years ago? They've improved them 200 percent since then."

I said that maybe Ed raises the best corn around year after year, in spite of his old planter, and that he'd bought some new boxes for it.

"Someday it's going to catch up with him. You wait. You can only run a piece of equipment so long and it'll break down right when you need it most. What's he got, 1,200 acres of corn and still fooling around with that old planter? If he'd pay more attention to his equipment and quit painting his goddamned buildings, he'd be better off. Say, what'd you want anyway?"

"Oh, nothin', just saw your new baler and thought I'd look at 'er up close."

"Yeah, well I can see why. They've got a new one comin' out next fall. It's got a built-in sensor that starts wrapping the bale at just the right time. Takes out all the guesswork. They're just going to make a few, so I'll have the only one around here."

*Most of the luxuries and
many of the so-called
comforts of life are not
only not indispensable, but
positive hindrances to
the elevation of mankind.*

Henry David Thoreau

God gave me my money.

John D. Rockefeller

Farmer Grable: Frugality as a Duty

Ike Grable is a throwback to seventeenth-century New England. He owns the first dollar he ever made, and he counts the day lost if he doesn't work up a sweat. Beyond this, he has struck a curious bargain with God whereby he pays God a percentage of his earnings every year and does not drink, smoke, or pursue fast women. In return, God protects his crops from hail and drought, his animals from disease, and slips Ike a few money-making opportunities now and then that he gives to no one else. If some disaster overtakes Ike, he can only assume God has screwed up, as all hired help is wont to do on occasion, and hope He will straighten up and tend to business in the future.

Believing deeply that God helps those that help themselves, Ike does his best to make his own luck. The theory is that hard work goes a long way toward creating good fortune, and the harder the work, the more fortune will eventuate. Thus Ike goes about making his work as difficult as possible. Most folks with two hundred acres of irrigated corn own grain augers to move the crop around from truck to bin and bin to truck. Grable scoops it all by hand. Most folks with a thousand head of fat cattle have some mechanical method of mixing the feed. Not Grable, who uses two 5-gallon buckets and a scoop shovel to mix cattle feed in each bunk.

While his neighbors were rushing out to buy $30,000 tractors that would do their farm work in half the time, Ike bought some new rings for his 1949 John Deere. He was upset that the dealer charged him twenty dollars. Long hours in the field don't bother him in the slightest; on the contrary, working from dawn to dusk is positively gratifying.

"Those new machines are probably all right if a man can afford them. I sure can't. Some of the boys have had trouble with 'em and repairs are expensive. If a man isn't workin', he's liable to get in trouble with liquor and so on. A feller just as well work a little harder and save a little money at the same time."

Last year Ike finally broke down and bought a small horsepower tractor for around ten thousand dollars. Folks thought he'd slipped a cog, but he had an explanation.

"They have this accountant over at the bank that does my taxes ever' year, an' he claimed the gummit would pick up half the cost of the tractor, what with depreciation and my showing some profit. So I went and bought it, and, sure enough, that young fellow was right. Two years from now the gummit will have bought and paid for that tractor. It doesn't make a lot of sense, but then the gummit never does. It isn't too bad a tractor either, even if it doesn't stack up with my A John Deere. That old A takes half the fuel. A man's got to watch his fuel bills anymore. They'll eat you up."

"Doesn't that new tractor make your field work go a lot faster?" I asked, hoping to catch Ike admitting he was working shorter hours and liking it.

"Oh, it probably would if I drove it in a fast gear. I tried that for a while, but she went so fast I couldn't see what I was doing, so I cut it down to first gear. A fellow shouldn't run over his fields so fast, he's liable to forget why he's out there."

I could see Grable's life-style wasn't going to be subverted by anything so trivial as a new tractor. In fact, there was a rumor around that he was going to sell it because the seat was too comfortable and he kept falling asleep at the wheel.

There has naturally been a considerable amount of speculation as to how Ike has been able to fight progress to a standstill and have money to show for it.

Shaky Ed holds the most popular theory: "Ike is so goddamned tight there ain't a nickel that he gits hold of that ever gits away. I've seen the sonofabitch reset the same post four or five times. As quick as one rots off, he turns her upside down, an' back in the ground she goes. Some of his fences are two feet tall, fer Chrissakes."

He loves to tell the story of how Ike once drove two hundred miles to catch back on a cup of coffee he'd been maneuvered into buying for a traveling salesman. When the time came to pay the check, Shaky Ed had hollered out that Ike was buying, and everyone filed out of the cafe before Ike realized what was going on. The whole bill came to eighty cents, and some witnesses claimed there was foam in Ike's mouth, but that's probably an exaggeration.

Ike's own explanation for his success is hard to come by, unless you happen to catch him coming out of the bank after a pilgrimage to his safety deposit box. Sometimes he mellows to the point where it's hard to shut him up.

"I think the main reason I've got some money that other boys don't have is that I was never scared of work. Man was made to work, you know. If you work hard, you can't get any bad habits started, like booze and loose wimmin. Hard work takes your mind off of frivolous things like television and politics so you can concentrate on farming and saving money.

"Another reason is that I don't buy a nail or a piece of machinery just because I need it. Some guys think nothing of going to town and picking up a four-dollar sack of nails. That would scare me. If I find myself short a nail or two and feel like taking an expensive trip to town, I kind of wait until the feeling passes. Pretty quick I usually remember where there's a board with a couple of fairly good nails in it. Maybe I have to straighten them out, but I haven't spent any money on gas or nails, and I've saved some working time besides. These guys that go to town all the time run an awful chance of bumping into some booze or a fast woman or two. A guy that stays home and works finds after a while that he doesn't really need to go at all. If I didn't have to come in here to bank and go to church, I'd save a lot of time and gas. I offered the church a piece of ground out here to put a new building on, but these soft folks in town thought it was too far to drive.

"Another reason for my hanging on to a little money is that God and I have a deal. I give Him 10 percent right off the top and He takes care of the markets and the weather. One time I gave him 9 percent by mistake, and He put green bugs on my wheat so thick they had it eaten down before I knew what was happening."

I asked Ike if just anybody could make an arrangement with God.

"No, as a matter of fact. I don't think there's too many that can do it. First of all, God doesn't like people that don't want to work, and that takes care of 90 percent of the population, unless you count Mexicans, and they're mostly Catholic and have a different god than we do. In the second place, God doesn't care for high living, new cars, or nice clothes, and that eliminates most of the rest of the people. I don't guess there's many of us that really get along too well with God, and it's a shame, because 10 percent is a cheap hired hand when you consider what you get in return."

I once asked Ike if he thought he could make it if he were starting over today with high land and low commodity prices.

"That's not too bad a question, sonny, and I've given it some thought. It would be harder. When I was your age and starting out, you could buy the best land around here for twenty dollars an acre, and we didn't have electricity and telephone bills eating us up every month. I think I'd get a good job and save my money. A young guy ought to be able to work a forty-hour week for someone else and have enough vinegar left to work another forty hours for himself. I'd probably either get a few milk cows or some sows and rent a farmstead for fifty bucks a month. In four or five years I could pay cash for a small place. If I had accumulated some equipment, like an A John Deere, a disc, and a drill, I could maybe rent some wheat ground. If I saved my profits, I could probably pay cash for a quarter section in another five years. Then I'd quit my job and start farming a little bigger. It would take awhile, but I'd get there. I wouldn't borrow money unless I had to, and then I wouldn't borrow it for very long. Borrowed money will break you sooner than anything. Guys like Ed are on their last legs. Eighteen percent interest is more than the best farmer can overcome. Of course if Ed worked a little harder and didn't spend his money foolishly on barn paint and liquor, he'd have a better chance. I don't know how he's stayed in business as long as he has. I couldn't do things that way and last a year. I've even heard that he spends good money on tractor wax. Nobody ever made a dime on shiny tractors. They don't impress God much either."

If you get the idea that God and Ike think pretty much alike, you wouldn't miss it by far. Perhaps that's the real reason for his success. It's hard to argue with a farmer with the Big Fellow in his pocket.

vertegration: The process of carrying any economic activity to its logical monopolistic conclusion, thereby corrupting and degrading all who participate.

Craig Van Boening,
The Spaceman's Dictionary of Agricultural Terminology

Organic Vertegration

Organic farming has gained adherents in the past twenty years. Most of the technology used is rather elderly, dating back to ancient China; however, some practices, such as organic pest management, are comparatively new. Basic organic practices, such as crop rotation, green-manure plowdown, and composting, are proven superior farming techniques and should not be controversial. The total abstinence from the use of chemicals, herbicides, pesticides, and fertilizers, as practiced by some organic zealots, is the issue that has generated most of the heat and very little of the light between pro- and antichemical farmers. Farmers who have mastered the use of Treflan and 2-4-D generally view organic farmers as left-wing weirdos who want to turn back the clock and cut yields for everyone. Organic farmers tend to perceive chemical farmers as backward sinners who, if they would only see the light, could grow bountiful crops without poisoning their farms or using a lot of high-cost petrochemicals. University researchers, who might be expected to resolve the fuss with some timely research, have only poured gasoline on the fire. Organic farmers believe that chemical companies have an undue influence on university research results and do not believe tests that reflect badly on organic practices. Prochemical farmers tend to believe university test results that reflect favorably on chemical methodology and to ignore evidence of organic superiority. Some folks in the organic camp believe that the high cost of commercial fertilizers and chemicals has made a switch in farming practices inevitable and that the rising cost of imported oil will force American farmers to go organic in the very near future. While there is no evidence that any big change is imminent, many farm communities now have an organic practitioner for the neighbors to study. Any successes will be noted, and if repeated often enough, imitation will follow.

The most successful organic farmers resemble successful chemical farmers in that they tend to be well established and in a position to take a few financial knocks without going under. Most farmers who have given up chemicals have suffered up to three years of lower yields, increased insect activity, and weed problems. Most say such difficulties abated in the fourth year of changeover, and then the milk and honey of healthy soil, balanced insect populations, and weed control through crop rotation began to take effect. Farmers laboring under a heavy debt load have a difficult time surviving one year of reduced income, let alone three. This is one reason for the popularity of organic farming among relatively well-heeled farmers and those just entering on a part-time basis. The latter often have another source of income and can afford to experiment.

My favorite organic farmer fits into neither of these categories. Tony needs to maximize farm income every year. If he doesn't, his creditors will force him into a different occupation. Tony's career as an organic farmer has been marked by one fiasco after another. First, the banker wasn't impressed with the new way of farming. "If it's such hot stuff, why isn't everyone doing it?" Then there were the inevitable bug and weed difficulties that reduced yields and confirmed the banker's suspicions. Living one mistake away from bankruptcy is not a particularly desirable position, and the pressure did not contribute to Tony's domestic tranquility. His wife, Thelma, reluctantly took an off-farm job to meet living expenses. There were dubious neighbors, like Shaky Ed, who bequeathed Tony forever the nickname "Organic Tony." At first, Tony patiently explained his views on nonchemical agriculture but gave up in the face of merciless banter. Working under a crushing debt load, Tony was locked into producing maximum cash returns. This led to a concentration on organic pinto beans, edible soybeans, and wheat. Some organic processors would orally contract for a truckload of organic pinto beans, only to drop the price or renege completely at harvest. Tony found himself marketing his production door-to-door at city health-food stores to obtain the prices he had counted on. His marketing costs were terrific and his net income fell below everybody's expectations.

"I felt I had reached the bottom. I had a thousand bushels of organic, edible soybeans and I couldn't find a store that would take over fifty pounds at a time. The banker wanted me to sell them at the elevator to pay off a note I had coming due. I knew I could get eighteen bucks for them somewhere, but I was running out of time. That's when Thelma thought up Organic Tony's Cosmic Cereal. I guess I oughta give Ed some of the credit, but Thelma really pushed it. We scraped up some money and took out an ad in a couple of national health magazines. Two months later I'd sold the whole works for twenty bucks a bushel, and the customers had paid the freight. Since then we've sold everything through the mail that we've raised. The banker smiles when he sees me, and we've been able to add some processing equipment without adding to our debt. I guess you could call it vertical integration, or vertegration, as Thelma says, although we're so small it doesn't seem appropriate. We grow the grain, process it, and market it, so there are absolutely no middlemen involved. We've got customers from as far away as Alaska that buy Organic Tony's Cosmic Cereal just like clockwork."

Some of us have tried a variety of Tony's organic products, with mixed results, but they all have flavor going for them, if nothing else. Thus far, Ed claims he hasn't eaten any of Tony's stuff. Says it leads to immorality and international communism. Some folks think Ed's just irritated because Tony turned his teasing into a nationwide brand name. Of course, it doesn't help when some of us greet Ed as "Mister Organic Marketing Genius." Ed has always lacked a certain ability to laugh at himself.

*I am wont to think that
men are not so much the
keepers of herds as herds
are the keepers of men, the
former are so much freer.*

Henry David Thoreau

*There's has-beens and there's
will-bes and then there's cows.**

Milton Tupper

* A "has been" is an old cow who probably doesn't raise much of a calf, who'll
likely drop over dead the first good excuse she gets. A "will be" is a first- or
second-calf heifer that may have trouble calving and probably won't give much
milk to her calf either. A cow is a four-to-seven-year-old animal that will likely
raise a calf every year and not die.

*All Cattlemen
Are Crazy*

There are many farmers in this country who have small herds of cattle to eat their rough pasture ground in the summer and their crop residues in winter. They generally try to get the cheapest possible investment involved in their calf crops. Other farmers occasionally feed cattle when corn is cheap, but it is definitely a sideline with them and quite often a money-losing proposition. A cattleman as defined here is a person who makes his primary income from cattle, be it the rancher who sells weaning calves or the feedlot operator who buys those calves and sells them as fat cattle.

What makes the cattleman so unusual is that, with the exception of possibly fifteen years out of the last hundred, he has always lost money on his investment. That this individual is not extinct is a real tribute to the romance attached to the cattle business and the consummate insanity of the people involved.

In the 1860s and early 1870s wild longhorn cattle were rounded up in Texas and New Mexico and driven north to Abilene, Dodge City, and Wichita. These cattle were essentially free for the taking or could be purchased for as little as four dollars a head from a rancher who had no local market for his product. Delivered in Kansas, they might fetch thirty to fifty dollars a head if they arrived early, or nothing if they arrived after the market had become glutted. Some went directly to the packers, others to Illinois and Indiana to be fattened, still others on north to Wyoming and Montana to stock new range country. This bonanza was relatively short-lived, and free grass and free cattle disappeared behind new fences of barbed wire. Expensive breeding stock was imported from England along with huge amounts of European capital. British interests bought up the largest ranches and launched ambitious breeding projects to improve their herds. The small rancher was pressured out of business by the methods documented in the standard Hollywood oater. The British quickly found out that there were few economies of size that could compete with low prices, ferocious blizzards, and incompetent or dishonest management.

What the law of supply and demand did to ranch interests was small potatoes compared to the effect of the sodbuster. Homesteaders wrecked the free-land concept that was the foundation of the early days of the cattle business. By first fencing in, then plowing the open range, farmers gradually eroded the great ranches to pitiful proportions. Some individual ranchers made money with government contracts for Indian reservations, but for the most part the industry lapsed into a permanent state of poor health. During the War Years of 1914–18, 1941–45, 1949–53, 1964–73, some real profits were made by individuals who came to the party early, bought cheap, and then had the foresight to sell out before the boom ended. Most operators gave back in spades whatever profits they made. Each war fueled high prices for breeding stock, pasture land, and grain. Those who bought high-priced land during good years, usually borrowing heavily to do so, saw its value wither away as the inevitable bust in cattle prices ruined its earning power. Breeding stock purchased at a premium often brought 10 cents on the dollar during the lags that followed. Recent history found feedlots full of 70-cent-a-pound calves bought in

1973 and fed on $3.50 corn selling for 35 cents in 1974. Cows worth $600 per head in 1973 plummeted to $70 by fall of 1975. Feedlot operators, believing that Nixon's price freeze on beef had brought on artificially low prices, loaded up on 45-cent calves in the spring of 1974, only to find out that the glut of beef was just beginning to hit the world. By mid-fall of 1975, old thin cows brought as little as 6 cents a pound in local sale barns, heifer calves changed hands at 11 cents a pound, and steers for 16 cents. Cow prices had dropped over 400 percent on average in less than two years, while hamburger prices in the stores fell less than 30 percent. At this point everyone stopped believing in Santa Claus. Bankers rid their portfolios of problem cattle loans, ranchers began to liquidate their herds, and feedlots around the country sprouted enormous crops of weeds. By 1977 small profits began to show up on the ledgers of cattle feeders, and a rosy outlook continued into spring of 1978. Prices reached and then passed their 1973 peaks. Cow-calf operators were looking at a break-even profit picture for the first time in five years. Then, led by a bespectacled freak by the name of Barry Bosworth, the Carter Administration singled out beef as the focal point for an attack on its self-induced inflation. Beef import quotas were expanded to allow large quantities of poor-quality foreign meat into the country. Hamburger cow prices fell $10 a hundred-weight in one week. Calf prices declined even more, in some cases $20 a hundred.

What sane human being would operate a business in conditions like these? A ranch stocked with a hundred head of brood cows will cost upwards of $250,000. That kind of dough would buy you some nice duplexes and maybe a car wash to look after. You could even put it out on interest and get $18,000 a year to make car payments. With a quarter of a million dollars invested in that ranch, you can stand in below-zero weather with your arm up a cow's ass, trying to grab her calf's other leg so you can pull him out and have him freeze to death.

You can watch that bull you paid $2,000 for breed your cows all summer using a pair of testicles that got frozen last winter so they don't work any more. Then you can wait for a calf crop that never comes. If you are a real masochist, you'll stick a hundred dollars worth of drugs into a sick cow, get her healthy, and have her walk into a pond and drown.

Had you paid cash for said ranch, your net return after real estate taxes, death loss, fence repair, trucking, and winter feed would have been around $7,000. That was before Mr. Bosworth tried to lead a consumer boycott of beef on the "Today" show. Lord help you if you'd borrowed any money at 16 percent. Let's see, $250,000 invested gets you a full-time job at $7,000 a year. Makes your mouth water, doesn't it? Less than 3 percent on your investment, and you get to work for free! Do you still doubt that cattlemen are crazy? There's more.

A friend of mine recently went belly-up as a cattle feeder. It had taken only two years to wipe out everything he had invested the previous thirty. He went to work as a cowboy for a large feedyard in the Middle West, owned by a couple of chain grocery stores. I went out to see him working on his new job. I expected him to have some adjustment problems after being his own boss for thirty years.

"How's it going?"

"Good, I've never made so much money in my life. It's damn near criminal what they pay me. I'm clearin' over $1,100 a month, and I only work twelve hours a day, six and a half days a week. Knowing how easy it is to make money workin' for somebody else, I wonder how come it took me so long to figure it out."

"Don't you miss being your own boss?"

"Nope, 'cause here I am my own boss. Nobody else knows shit from shinola and inside of a year I'm gonna be running this place." (It took him six months.)

"You oughta see what they get for help around here. These

guys don't give a damn about cattle, they think they oughta go home at six like everybody else. They bitch and moan about working on Sundays, half the time they call in sick. If a critter's sick, they don't even notice the poor sonafabitch till he's dead. I've got to kick ass all day just to get stuff fed. It's a mess, is what it is."

"How do these guys make any money feeding cattle if it's so bad?"

"Well, that's a damned good question. I think maybe they like not having to buy their beef on the open market. Then I'm sure there's a tax break in it. They can lose money on this lot and charge it off against what they make on the stores, or they can pay themselves a whole wad for their fat cattle and then lose money on the store. It's too damned complicated for me to figure out, but they seem to be able to pay a whole bunch of dumbasses to sit around out here and do nothin'. Then they do a little custom feedin'. Some rancher will bring in a pen of cattle, and they'll charge him ten cents a day per head yardage and whatever the feed bill is. They mark the feed up around 30 percent over what it costs them. They always have a 3 percent death loss on the cattle they take in. Say a guy brings in two hundred head to feed. Well, about the time they get fat, the manager calls him and tells him six of his steers just died. That way the manager pays for all their feed and the grocery store gets 'em for nothing. We shipped two semiloads out last night that was nothing but them dead 3 percenters. That's what we call 'em. I imagine them grocery stores gotta work real hard to lose money on free cattle."

"This is a mighty big place compared to most feedlots. How many do you handle at once?"

"Oh, about 100,000 head. I tell you the funniest damn thing keeps happening. We get these guys comin' out here about my age, and they ask me if they can look at the cattle, and I say "Sure." They stand and stare at them steers for maybe an hour or so, and I get to jabberin' with 'em, and I find out they're busted cattle feeders just like me. They just miss being around fat cattle, so they come out here to look at some. Ain't that the damnedest thing you ever heard of? 'Course, I gotta admit if I'd have quit feedin' cattle cold turkey and hadn't got this job, I'd probably be doin' the same thing, beggin' my way into some big outfit's feedlot, so I could moon at the fat cattle."

Quitting cold turkey? That sounds like a bad drug habit or maybe like an alcoholic. What is it about cattle that gets people hooked to the point where they'll turn their life savings literally into one big manure pile?

Maybe it's all those trips out to the pasture in the spring, seeing little calves hiding in the grass, or butting on one another, or running down the hill trying their new legs out. Maybe it's walking through the herd at dusk in the summertime, hearing all that munching and cud-chewing and pure, unadulterated contentment. Maybe it's bringing a bunch of cold, hungry critters through a snowstorm by shoveling snow all day so they can eat enough hay to get them by. Maybe it's watching your whole year's wages be decided on one day out of the year when your calves go through the auction ring, and you're hoping the buyers are there and not asleep, and the auctioneer brags up your cattle as being something special, and maybe you half believe him, and maybe, just maybe, this year you top the sale. Maybe it's starting a pen of weak-looking scrubby cattle on corn, treating the sick ones, willing them to eat, and seeing them six months later fat and glossy, playing games with birds in the lot, looking like some ideal picture on a steak house wall, thinking about how some lucky housewife might get to buy a piece of good meat for a change because you put it on the counter with your sweat and your worry.

Cattlemen are incurable romantics. They trust in free enterprise, better prices next year, and believe deeply they will outlast the Barry Bosworths of this world. Who's got the heart to tell them that for every man that truly loves cattle, there's two thousand Barry Bosworths just dying to make a career out of making life miserable for them? Government intervention in the cattle market continues to trouble producers. As inflation further erodes consumer buying power, the cattle business may well find itself as the main whipping boy for every congressman who enjoys prime-rib dinners at the taxpayers' expense but feels average Americans would be ahead in health and wealth buying less expensive, formaldehyde-packed chickens.

In the final analysis the cattle business contains an inordinate amount of risk and requires huge amounts of capital. It has been and will remain largely a rich man's game. Our present tax structure will ensure that Wall Street cowboys will continue to put cattle in feedlots and that movie stars will own cattle ranches at staggering yearly losses. In all probability Big Mac attacks will be assuaged, and chain steak houses will continue to proliferate. What is not clear is whether the small cattle producer will survive into the twenty-first century. His extinction might create some interesting repercussions. If, for instance, the vast majority of cattle become the property of those looking for a tax shelter, would not those cattle raisers become insulated from the law of supply and demand? If they lost money this year, that is all to the good. It will save them money on our tax bill. In fact, it might not even be necessary to produce a very terrific calf crop year after year. They can still depreciate the cows and the fences. If prices are good they might unload some brood cows and take some capital gains. If prices are bad they may switch to the inventory method of figuring taxes and get a bigger loss than they could by selling. When a producer who depends on cattle for his livelihood runs into low prices, the reaction usually is to liquidate the herd. When prices are good he usually increases numbers, thereby holding that beef off the market. If we reach the point where most cattle are owned by dentists, movie stars, and successful talk-show hosts, the cattle cycle as we have known it may indeed be over. Instead of a graph showing peaks and valleys, there may be a line rising steadily to the upper right hand corner. Consumers might see the percentage of their disposable income spent on meat double and triple. The Ralph Nader of that time, whoever he may be, will gnash his teeth, but he will surely be as impotent as he'd be if he attacked the great oil companies. Should any independent cattlemen survive to see such a state of affairs, their financial affairs should improve dramatically. To be both crazy and solvent would be a situation some folks might envy. To a cattleman it would be heaven on earth.

*We always called hogs
the mortgage raisers,
and they were.*

B. J. Tupper

Harry the Hog Man

Farmers complain constantly. They complain about weather, be it too cold or too hot, too wet or too dry. They wish it would freeze so they could harvest their corn, and they hope it doesn't before the milo has matured. Farm prices are so high they are bound to be the ruination of the country, or they are so low as to bust every farmer inside of a month. If the government would only keep its nose out of their business they could make a living, especially if it would raise the loan price another fifty cents a bushel and maybe put on some decent-sized acreage controls.

Often complaining becomes a form of reverse bragging. "How am I supposed to get 1,200 acres of corn in with all this rain?" tells the listener this man has a sizeable operation. "My Steiger runs so goddamned bad I think I'll take it back to the factory and tell them to shove it" lets us in on the news that the storyteller has a new eighty-thousand-dollar tractor that he would throw back in the dealer's lap rather than put up with a little poor engine performance.

Harry the Hogman seldom complains. In a crowd of angry farmers, he stands serene. From time to time he may voice some small protest ("Sure is cold, ain't it?") so as to fit in with the crowd, but his performance is unconvincing. Optimism and goodwill bubble out as if from some great artesian well. Why is this man smiling? It's the nature of his business.

If corn prices are high, Harry knows hog numbers will go down and prices will go up. A low corn price means he is now making good money, and even if the values deteriorate at some inevitable future date, today there is a profit. Disease can wipe out a whole pig crop. Two or three hundred little dead pigs can drive a grown man to drink before noon. But if the disease is cutting his production, it most probably is going through swine herds all over the neighborhood, maybe the whole country. Fewer pigs mean higher prices. He has only to wait four months for a new pig crop, and next time his stock should be immune. There is no better medicine for a disastrous farrowing than a healthy litter of ten or twelve lively little pigs the next time around.

Harry sells hogs every week, fifty-two weeks a year. His cash flow is impressive. Bills do not hang over his head, nor does he have money borrowed for any length of time. Unlike the cow-calf man, who must wait an entire year to recoup his investment, Harry gets his returned continously in large chunks.

The cattleman may make his annual shipment of cattle, only to find he has picked the worst market of the year. A whole year must pass before he can hope to recover his losses. By marketing hogs every week, Harry gets in on his share of lows, but he also hits the highs. Over the past ten years hog prices have rarely stayed below profitable levels for an entire year. Harry took a bath with everyone else in 1969–70 and in 1974. July of 1974 was Black Friday for the hog business. Harry took 19 cents a pound for four loads of fat hogs (40 head to a load). He lost $31 per head, or $4,960. Contrast this sad picture with the cattle feeder in 1974 who was losing $150 per head. One hundred sixty head of fat cattle in 1974 lost him a cool $24,000. While his neighboring cattle feeders were mortgaging their farms and driving last year's cars, Harry lost $12,000, largely because of his living expenses. His hog business was essentially a break-even proposition.

Over the past ten years Harry has done very well, thank you. His overall net return on invested capital has been just short of 80 percent. For a man who lives on just $15,000 per year, this can mean lots of spending money.

The obvious question is why aren't more people raising hogs? Hogs are destructive, sometimes evilly intelligent, and blessed with a unique aroma. Sows are prone to eat their pigs, lie on their pigs, stop giving milk to their pigs, and charge viciously toward anyone who may want to help. They are inclined to be anywhere they are not supposed to be. At Harry's farm, "The pigs are out!" means that all available hands are galvanized into frenzied action. Hog roundups can be most frustrating and have resulted in a few divorces over the years. No one has kept track of hog-inspired murders and suicides.

These innate characteristics of hogs have brought about modern pork plants that rely on concrete and steel to minimize frustration. There is a sizeable body of scientific evidence that says efficient hog producers should raise hogs in confinement. A growing percentage of hogs is being raised in this manner, often by corporations resembling the vertically integrated broiler operations that spelled doom for chicken enterprises on the family farm. Subsidized by favorable tax laws, producing a steady flow of nonfarm capital investment by doctors, lawyers, merchants, and thieves, and using the benefits of millions of dollars worth of land-grant university research, corporate hog operations threaten the existence of small-scale hog ventures. The corporate swine activity is not necessarily more efficient nor inherently more profitable. On the contrary, only tax advantages allow the modern pork plant to compete with the average hog farmer. However, the death blow to small-farm hog production will come from the two tendencies of vertically integrated farm enterprises that killed the small-farm poultry business: production and contract marketing. Corporate sow facilities maintain constant numbers regardless of market price fluctuations. Their tax advantages and abundant capital insulate them from mundane short-term profit-and-loss considerations. Automakers will shut down plants when faced with a burdensome supply of cars. It is almost impossible to temporarily close a hog factory because of the high cost of breeding stock suitable for confinement and the lag time caused by the gestation period of sows. This means that during periods of oversupply, hog factories will continue to pour their product onto the market. As the number of small producers dwindles, periods of decreased hog numbers will be few and far between. The erratic swings in supply over the years have made the hog business profitable for the shrewd small-scale operator. However, he may survive the pressure on prices caused by consistently large hog slaughter if the packers don't lock out his production. More long-term contracts between packing houses and corporate hog factories will be signed. Eventually most existing slaughter facilities will be tied up with the processing of contracted animals. Much as the egg market is now controlled by the supermarket chains, future hog markets may exist only in Wilson and IBP computers.

None of these dire developments bother Harry. He has a confinement farrowing house that he built ten years ago for $15,000. It keeps his sows warm in winter and cool in summer. The manure collected underneath is an important part of Harry's fertilizer program. He has confidence in his flexibility. "Hogs were never meant to be raised on concrete. They go lame, they get nervous, they chew on one another, and they're starved for dirt. That's why my sows run on dirt except for the ten weeks a year they're in the farrowing house. My fat hogs get out on dirt when they weigh about 60 pounds, and we switch them to a clean lot at about 160 pounds. I have a whole bunch of fence to keep up 'cause we let each pen go fallow for six months a year. My feed conversion isn't quite as good as some of the better confinement units, but my rate of gain is better, and the hogs are just plain more content. A happy hog ain't going to die on you. Besides, if I want to quit raisin' hogs, all I got to do is hang up my fence pliers and walk away. I've got less than $5,000 invested in all the hog facilities outside the farrowing house. A fancy labor-saving set up would cost me $100,000. I can't afford that kind of money."

Contented hogs? Prefers to work on fence rather than invest some of his extra money in labor-saving equipment? Hasn't this man ever heard of progress? It's a cinch nobody from *Successful Farming* is going to look him up for a four-page feature with glossy color photographs.

"Yeah, I know my operation wouldn't impress any of the smart boys. Fact is, most years I make a little money. My risks are low, and I get a good return on my investment. Someday these FDA people may ban antibiotics in hog feed. By switching hogs to clean lots and keeping my sow herd closed I could survive. Maybe pork would get high enough a fella could afford to raise it.

"The big boys in the hog business have two disadvantages. They have no control over their energy and labor costs, both of which are likely to inflate rapidly. There may come a time in the near future when I start farrowing once or twice a year down on the river. I've visited a farmer that pasture-farrows, and his energy and labor costs are minimal. He also saves one hell of a lot on sow feed.

"Large confinement complexes are extremely vulnerable to some new disease epidemics. A whole operation could be wiped out overnight. Your big boys don't like high-strung, active hogs, so most of them have Yorkshire and Landrace crosses, breeds especially adapted to the prison condition of uptown confinement farrowing. The modern hog has had most of the natural healthy meanness bred out of him. If the

pork industry keeps trying to turn the hog into an indoor animal with a pleasant disposition, we're going to have massive
disease outbreaks. I've got a cousin in Tennessee that knows a
guy with some ugly, nasty hogs that have never seen a barn. If
I could get some of them, I might start breeding a little natural
meanness back into my own hogs. It'll help them survive when
I turn them out in the river bottom. This is how I plan to
compete with the big boys, and I think you'll see more fellows
going this route."

Like most hog men, Harry is conscious of his social obliga-
tions. Where the cattleman and the sheep man tend to resemble their nomadic forerunners, the hog man looks on society
as both a tool and an obligation.

"Sure, I've served on the school board and the State Pork
Council and even thought of running for county commissioner, but those jobs don't pay anything, and I'm not a politician by any means. Maybe I've got more money than the next
guy and can afford the time a little better. But somebody has
got to see things are run right. The hog business has a product
to sell, and we need to keep the public informed about what
we offer. It's easy to sell pork because we give good value. A
housewife can make a ten-pound ham last one hell of a lot
longer than ten pounds of almost any meat you can name. A
pork chop is tasty whether it comes off an old sow or a prize-
winning fat hog. You can't say that about beef or chicken. An
old hen tastes, by god, like an old hen, and a steak off an old
cow isn't going to be very tender. One of these days these
quack doctors are going to discover that vegetable oils aren't
what they're cracked up to be and that cholesterol is good for
people, and then a fella can afford to raise pork. Meanwhile,
we'll have to do the best job of sellin' we can. I feel sorry for
the consumer stuck with a nine-to-five job and a pay check. He
gets cut every way there is, and chances are food is the one
place he has to scrimp. I wish everyone could eat as well as we

do. I know there would be happier people on this earth if everyone got three squares, and I ain't talking about a dab of cottage cheese and a can of some damned diet pop as being a meal. People that need the most food can't afford it, and that's about as bassakwards as you can get. What we oughta do is give them folks food stamps for real honest-to-god food, like meat, milk, flour, eggs, stuff like that. Now they're buying candy and soft drinks. I'd like to see them increase the food stamp program and cut out the frill buying for six months on a trial basis. I'll bet most of these people wouldn't be able to eat all the food they could afford to buy, and I'll bet the price of pop and candy would find a way to come down. It doesn't make much sense to have the government buy up surplus milk products to hold the price up and at the same time give folks food stamps so they can go out and buy soda pop, which is bad for 'em. If people were as smart as hogs are about eating, it wouldn't be a problem."

Harry is twenty-eight years old, but he has some thoughts about retiring early.

"Well, you can only spend so much money, you know? While I'm working it's hard to get away, and it's hard to hire good help. I think maybe in a few years I'll hang 'er up, at least for a while. There's a big ol' world out there. I'd like to see some of those ugly Chinese hogs that have twenty pigs to the litter and talk to some of those Common Market farmers and find out how they got in so good with their governments. I'm taking French at the college, and I'm going to try German next semester. Maybe I'll find out something over across the pond that'll help me decide what to do with the rest of my life. Probably it'll have something to do with hogs. They've been good to me and I like 'em."

I never owned any sheep.
To make a living you'd
have to have a couple of
thousand of 'em and
that's a lot of baa-baas.

B. J. Tupper

Slumming with Sheep

Owning sheep is not one of your major status symbols in this country. In the rural community it is regarded as considerably less than that. It is a very similar situation to that of the successful surgeon who complains that his garbage man makes more money than he does but does not then rush out and buy a garbage truck. The sheep business, like the garbage business, has some odious connotations. Sheep are regarded as stupid, smelly, and quite likely to die for no reason. Sheep men reinforce the prejudice by wearing oil-caked hats and driving ancient pickup trucks. Indeed, within the sheep industry the folks with the cruddiest, sloppiest hats and the most rust-encrusted pickups are regarded as very superior fellows. Red 1952 Chevy pickups with wood stock racks and spotlights are the vehicles of choice, although there are some die-hard Studebaker drivers out there who are downright snobbish.

A true sheep man is one tough sonofabitch. Compared with a sheep man, most cattlemen and hog men are lily-livered weaklings. Corn farmers do not even compute. Maybe it's because sheep are so delicate that they demand rough character from their owners. Keeping alive an animal so totally stupid as a sheep certainly requires more intelligence and skill than is necessary in caring for most other animals. Sheep must be protected from overeating, not eating enough, running en masse off a cliff, and being eaten by dogs and coyotes. Ewes reject their lambs at a worrisome rate, and the resulting bum lambs must be raised on the bottle. A sudden noise may cause a prize buck to drop dead from shock. Ewes develop mastitis or "bag trouble" frequently and may not give enough milk for one lamb, let alone two. Sheep never go where they're supposed to, unless they all go at once. Anyone who tries to load or unload sheep at night usually ends up carrying each sheep on or off. Shearing sheep is such back-breaking work that it quickly imparts a permanent stoop to those few folks that still practice the trade. These difficulties have dramatically reduced the large flocks found in the western states. Small-farm sheep production has swelled in recent years, but not enough to offset the losses in the range country. Consequently, the sheep business has been the most consistently profitable livestock industry in the country for the past thirty years. Where the good hog man may make some money seven out of ten years, the cattleman one year in ten, the dairyman six in ten, the turkey raiser three in ten, the sheep man whips along year after year marking up tidy profit margins. This is largely because of the productivity of sheep as a species and the low capital requirements for entrance into the business. In addition, where it is perfectly acceptable for a sheep man to drive a vehicle worth $150 outside top, cattlemen feel compelled to drive this year's four-wheel-drive model and lay out a few more bucks for a Buick or Oldsmobile to drive to church. Sheep men don't go to any church I know of. They don't permit themselves the extravagance. Small amounts of money count little to a man who has to spend thousands in an attempt to make a living, but to a sheep man, a couple of insignificant additions to the collection plate could be spent on breeding stock that would put money in his pocket. This is not to say that all sheep men are skinflints; it's just that they quite likely have their priorities in a different form from everyone else.

Sheep do not eat much compared with their flashier bovine cousins. Where one cow grazes, five or six ewes could make out very well. One ton of hay would keep an average Hereford cow for about two months. That same ton would feed a ewe for well over a year.

A cow herd, if very well managed, will produce a 90 percent calf crop every year. That is, for every ten cows in the herd, nine calves will be weaned. A moderately well-managed flock of sheep will produce a 120 percent lamb crop, and it is not unusual in some herds to reach the 150 percent level. This is because sheep bear twin lambs fairly often and triplets occasionally. The recent introduction of Finnish Landrace sheep may pave the way for 200 percent lamb crops in the future. Purebred Finnish Landrace sheep throw three to five lambs consistently. Usually they are weak and require supplemental feeding. However, when crossed with more common breeds (Rambouillet, Dorset, Suffolk, Hampshire), the resulting half-blood Finn ewe can produce two sturdy lambs each year.

Some producers have successfully accelerated their lambing schedules and are getting two crops of lambs per year. Because the gestation period of sheep is five months, and because sheep do not breed well in hot weather, this procedure means lambing in January, weaning in March, and hopefully getting the flock bred back so it will lamb in August. Two lamb crops per year would more than double income because maintenance expense would be virtually the same whether there was one crop or two.

Wool has benefited in price from the increased price of oil and a corresponding increase in the cost of synthetic fibers. A few years ago the expense of shearing almost canceled out the money received for the wool. Today wool sales can account for a significant portion of a sheep man's income. The government pays a support price on wool, which represents the difference between the average wholesale price and the government target price. Each January wool growers go to their local Agricultural Stabilization and Conservation office with the receipts from the wool they have marketed during the previous year. Also included will be any lambs sold in the wool (with wool unshorn). Some little government gnomes will then compute the average price received on wool for the year and determine the payments due each producer. In the spring, wool payments will be mailed out for the prior marketing year. A farm flock of 400 head will produce roughly 2,800 pounds of wool. If lambs are sold in the wool, an additional 2,400 pounds will be eligible for subsidy.

Edwin runs a small sheep ranch in north central Kansas. He runs 1,000 head of one-quarter Finn ewes and consistently produces a 150 percent lamb crop. He rents a thousand acres of pasture each year at $20 per acre. This feeds his ewes until early November. Edwin figured out it was cheaper to rent grass than to own it. He bought forty acres ten years ago with a good set of buildings for $200 an acre. He financed 80 percent of the purchase price with the Federal Land Bank for thirty years at 9¼ percent. His yearly payment is $608 per year. His real estate taxes are $80. On thirty of his forty acres Edwin raises irrigated corn, which he turns into corn silage. His production costs run about $150 per acre, or $4,500. Edwin's entire machinery inventory, with the single exception of his irrigation equipment, was purchased in used, but good condition. Edwin says he would never buy a used silage cutter if he had to do it over. He has spent over $600 on repairs for it, but now feels it will last him a good while. The entire initial cost of Edwin's machinery inventory was $16,000.* For $16,000 you can maybe buy the tires for a new four-wheel-drive tractor. If Edwin had not paid cash for his machinery, he would be paying interest at 18 percent, or $2,880 per year. Edwin's machinery has not depreciated noticeably since he bought it. In fact, some pieces are now worth more than he paid.

To supplement his silage Edwin must buy protein, which cost him $800 last year. He also bought corn to creep-feed his lambs, to the tune of $1,000. He bought five full-blood Finn rams, which set him back an additional $800. Veterinary bills and drugs added $600. His custom-shearing bill was $1,200. Thus, his total production costs were $21,000. He sold 1,300 head of fat lambs weighing 110 pounds each at 72 cents a pound, or $79.20 each. After trucking and selling commission, he netted $77.00 each, or $100,100. He kept 200 ewe lambs for breeding and sold 200 old ewes, which netted him $7,000. He sold 9,000 pounds of wool at 65 cents a pound and received $5,850. His government wool check arrived for $2,970. With a gross income of $115,920, Edwin had expenses of $21,000, resulting in a net income of $94,920. Edwin increased his net worth by the $300 in principal that he paid on his farm and by the inflation of land values, which added $8,400 to the value of his farm. Edwin's $94,920 in disposable income was essen-

---

*Edwin owns an A John Deere with an old-style Farmhand loader for which he paid $750 in 1970. He uses this machine both for loading his silage wagon, bought in 1972 for $800, and for loading manure in the spring. His manure spreader cost $125 in 1969. For field work Edwin uses a John Deere 730 for which he paid $2,500 in 1974. He has a 13½ foot disc bought in 1974 for $450, a four-row planter bought in 1974 for $300, a four-row cultivator also bought in 1974 for $225, a single-row silage cutter bought in 1975 for $950, two four-wheel silage trailers with hydraulic lifts bought in 1975 for $350 each, and a four-row hiller bought in 1974 for $250. In addition he owns eight hundred feet of six-inch aluminum irrigation pipe bought in 1974 for $1,000, an irrigation pump and motor, which, with the hole in the ground, cost him $8,000 in 1974.

tially just that. He has very few costly bad habits. He chews tobacco (cost $83.20 per year), drinks three quarts of whisky per year (cost $18), chops all the wood that heats his home (cost 0), pumps all his home and livestock water from two windmills (cost $13.20 in repairs), runs one 1952 Chevy pickup (cost $85 insurance, $10 in tire repair, $3 in oil, $260 in fuel), eats his own lamb, the produce of his garden, which his wife puts up every year, and the milk, butter, cheese and ice cream from his two milk cows, which he feeds silage year round. Edwin buys two pairs of boots, $70; four pairs of jeans, $50; four shirts, $24; and 12 pairs of socks, $15, every year. This keeps both him and his wife fully clothed. Edwin's hat is fifteen years old, and he has no plans to buy another. Edwin also bought coffee worth $150, flour worth $50, yeast worth $3, sugar worth $30, laundry detergent worth $30, and electricity worth $300. Edwin does not believe in the telephone. His total cash outlay for living expense was $1,194.00, leaving $93,726 to put in the bank at 14 percent interest. Since 1975 Edwin has banked $90,000 per year just like a slot machine.

Edwin pays no income or social security taxes because he feels the government is foolish with its money. IRS agents have been alerted every year by a computer that Edwin has not filed a tax return on his wool check. Once they drove in the yard, only to be discouraged by Marie, Edwin's stock dog. The next two years they drove by without stopping. They were not impressed with Edwin's ability to pay any taxes even if he owed some. Every year after that, they didn't drive out but wrote up reports saying they had and that Edwin was hopelessly broke.

Neither Edwin nor his wife has ever had any medical expense. Edwin does not believe in doctors. "Ninety percent are quacks and the other 10 percent are so busy a man could die just waiting to git in to see 'em."

Edwin credits his good fortune to staying out of doctors' offices: ("Best place in the world to pick up germs.") and the

"The ONE newsletter every Christian should be reading."

Christian Book Distributors

The **Voice** of the **Martyrs**

BUSINESS REPLY MAIL

FIRST-CLASS MAIL   PERMIT NO. 311   BARTLESVILLE, OK

POSTAGE WILL BE PAID BY ADDRESSEE

THE VOICE OF THE MARTYRS
1815 SE BISON RD
BARTLESVILLE OK 74006-9901

fact that his wife has had no children. "You want to screw up
female plumbing all you got to do is have it carry a kid or two.
It won't stand the strain." Not that Edwin regrets not having
children. "A doctor would probably charge $100 just to deliver
the damn thing, and I ain't never seen a kid that was worth
$100 to anyone but himself."

His net worth would look like this.

	Liabilities	*Assets*
40-acre farm bought in 1968 for $8,000	$5,334.00	$80,000.00
Equipment bought for $16,000	-0-	19,000.00
Sheep raised himself	-0-	50,000.00
Cash in the bank	-0-	390,000.00
	$5,334.00	$539,000.00
Net Worth		$533,666.00

Edwin is worth over a half-million dollars. If he walked
through the streets of one of our major cities, he would probably run a fifty-fifty chance of being picked up for vagrancy.
His neighbors view him with a combination of distaste and
pity. Obviously no one would choose to live like Edwin if he
had a choice. A few good-hearted souls have even left little care
packages of food on Edwin's doorstep late at night. Edwin
enjoys the food and mentally marks the sender down as a real
ding-dong. Edwin can buy and sell 90 percent of the people in
this country, but no one knows that because he doesn't do it.

He lives secure in the knowledge that sheep are white gold and he is one of the few who know it. He hopes the Jewish population of New York will proliferate and continue to eat lamb at Passover. No government agencies mess with his business because they have never viewed it as being important. He accepts his wool check with good grace every year as further proof of his astute choice of careers. He views political affairs as a waste of time and will not spend hard-earned gas money to go vote. The last preacher that showed up on Edwin's doorstep got a dose of what a Queensland Blue Heeler can do if sufficiently aroused. They claim it took thirty-five stitches to fix up the preacher's leg. Volunteers canvassing for Cancer Research, the Heart Fund, or the March of Dimes don't stop anymore. Salesmen stop only once, and then briefly. In short, Edwin has it made and no one knows it. For him, that is as close to being in heaven as he will ever get.

*I never made much money
milking cows except what I
saved because I couldn't
go anywhere and spend any.*

B. J. Tupper

Modern Slavery
in the
World of Milk

During the first half of the century, many farm families made their living expenses by selling cream and eggs. Saturday nights brought farmers into town to "trade" and catch up on local news. At the grocery store a ten-gallon can of cream and two cases of eggs would usually buy groceries for a week, with money left over for a pair of shoes and maybe a new dress. A dozen eggs brought as much as sixty cents wholesale in the mid-1920s. Today eggs are twenty-two cents a dozen when they're high. The egg business, one of the long-term foundations of the small family farm, was obliterated by competition from huge egg factories, often owned by grocery chains. Some California supermarkets own layer operations that turn out 150,000 dozen eggs a day. The grocery stores pay their egg subsidiaries sixty-five cents a dozen, thereby netting the subsidiaries tidy profits, which may be taxed at a low rate due to investment tax credit and accelerated depreciation. After the egg operations have outlived their accelerated depreciation schedule, they may drop their egg price to fifty-five cents, raising retail profits for the supermarkets and leaving the egg operations with untaxable deficits.

Since many stores no longer need enter the free market to purchase eggs, the price of "real farm" eggs has fallen to levels that make small-scale egg production a sorry proposition. In areas where customers bother to drive to the farm to purchase eggs, some small laying flocks survive. At sixty-five to eighty-five cents a dozen, farmers can make a little money. A few stubborn poultry raisers have contracted with local school lunch programs and nursing homes to provide eggs at a slightly lower cost than those at the grocery stores. These local markets are generally available in rural communities but would support only one or two modest layer operations in any given area. Any overproduction must be sold off wholesale, usually as breaking eggs at twenty-two cents a dozen. (Breaking eggs turn into powdered eggs and then into cake mixes and other handy little packages that run around a dollar and a half a pound.) Twenty-two cents a dozen is not a price to encourage egg production even on the most efficient poultry farm.

The cream business lived on for a few years after small-farm egg production died but fell victim to oleomargarine, the cholesterol quacks, and a government system of price supports that did nothing for the price of whole cream. Prices paid by creameries remain essentially the same as those paid in 1942. Most creameries no longer produce butter but have turned their machinery over to making oleomargarine. Butter is mainly produced as a by-product of the processing of whole fluid milk into nonfat dry milk. Farm cream production is largely an anachronism. The practice of running whole milk through a separator, the skim milk fed to livestock* and the cream sold for hard cash, used to be standard operating procedure on many small farms. Today whole-milk production is the name of the game. This subjects the producer to a whole range of government regulations that require large capital in-

---

* Skim milk can be used to raise small calves and to supplement the diets of pigs and laying hens. Skim milk replaces some protein requirements and often makes poor doers blossom. Hens that normally do not lay eggs in severe weather may return to production if skim milk is added to the diet.

vestment. With Grade A dairy barns running thirty to ninety thousand dollars and cows from nine to eighteen hundred, it has become difficult to start up on a shoe string.

Gerald and Sarah Wembly overcame the odds and built their dairy herd from scratch. They began farming on a rented quarter section. She taught school the first few years while her husband worked for the local cement plant nights and ran a few small-scale livestock projects on the side (ten sows, a dozen beef cows, a Christmas duck project that left him holding the bag on fifty unsold quackers, and a dozen baby Holstein heifer calves). He says that the schedule was rough but that his future plans made the long hours more bearable.

"Sarah and I wore out several pencils, but it always came back to milking cows. We couldn't afford to jump right in so we set goals, bought heifer calves, and saved some money. About four months before our oldest heifers were supposed to drop their calves we were able to buy a poor quarter section with a Grade B* milk barn for a good price on long-term contract. Naturally, we assumed by the time we got settled, the heifers would be making our living."

Gerald had made one small mistake. He had raised his heifers on the bottle in pens of four to six head. After he had fed the calves, the always hungry little critters had turned to each other for solace and had sucked on the small teats of their friends until they were scarred and ruined for milk production. As each heifer freshened, Gerald discovered she possessed at most two working teats. His three years of planning, saving, and hard work looked wasted.

"We almost gave it up right there, but we had too many chips in the pot to fold. We kept the baby heifer calves as they came, sold the baby bulls, and sold the cows for hamburger. It

---

* Officially Grade B is manufacturing grade milk used largely for cheese and requires a lower investment in buildings and equipment to meet inspection standards than Grade A.

like to broke my heart watching those girls go off to Mc-
Donald's like that, but there wasn't any other way. We put the
babies in individual pens. One go round with ruined bags was
enough, and we went looking for cheap milk cows. We must
have sorted through fifty cows that first year to get a dozen to
milk. There were high kickers, sneaky kickers, old gummers,
low-producers, no producers, bad bags, cronic mastitis—you
name it, we had it. As quick as we found a dud she went to the
Great Big Mac in the Sky and we went out and got a couple
more. Through it all we held our money together. Some of the
rejects sold for less than we had paid, while some brought considerably more. When the smoke cleared we had fifteen head
of cows that averaged thirty-four pounds of milk, and our milk
barn had some new holes kicked through the siding. Our
monthly income after feed costs was around $600.

"We limped along for a couple of years before the baby
heifer calves we'd raised came on stream. We kept culling, raising our performance standards, and using artificial breeding to
give us access to superior production potential. I guess you
could say we've got a pretty darn good herd now. We'll average
around fifty-six pounds per cow, and we've got high hopes for
a real set of heifers that are going to drop calves next spring.
They might raise our average ten to fifteen pounds over the
next few years."

I once asked Gerald why he had saddled himself with a job
that required him to work seven days a week with no time off
for good behavior. He'd obviously thought about it.

"There are several sound financial reasons, but the real reason is a little difficult to explain. If I had worked this hard for
this long selling waterless cookware door-to-door, I'd probably be hauling down some major bucks, so it really isn't
purely financial. Maybe I just like milking cows. Milk cows are
smart. They have individual personalities just like people. They
always get a little distressed before milking time, having full

bags and all. When we milk them they seem sort of relieved. They depend on us to do that, so I suppose we feel important. I don't know, maybe ask Sarah, it's hard to explain, like I said."

Family dairies usually contain from thirty to seventy-five cows and involve most members of the family in the labor force. Actual milking time will vary depending on the size of the herd and the sophistication of the facilities. A minimum of six man-hours a day, seven days a week is devoted to actually milking the cows. Additional time must be spent feeding the cows and replacement heifers and in cleaning equipment and facilities. These chores are relentless in nature. They must be done each day of the year and must be done by a person of some competence. It would be foolhardy indeed to turn over the care of a $1,500 cow to an untrained novice. Besides all of this, there will be field work to produce feed for the cows, manure removal, and fence mending that go with livestock operations. Mastitis is a constant threat to any milk cow, as are the dangers of hardware death, pneumonia, bloat, milk fever, and grass tetany. Dairy calves are especially susceptible to scours and pneumonia, and a high death rate is not uncommon. Many dairies have turned to artificial insemination to improve their herds. This increases labor requirements, necessitating constant herd monitoring to catch cows in heat for breeding. The obvious question is why would anyone milk for a living?

The answer lies partially in the cash flow. A milk check comes to the farm every week or two. This money represents in most instances full market price for any homegrown grain and roughage that went into making the milk, plus a return to labor and capital. Thus the dairyman is able to roll over his investment much more rapidly than a cash grain farmer or a cattleman. Because alfalfa and silage would be excellent cash crops in themselves if there weren't certain marketing and transportation problems in both, the return of market price for these items through the sale of milk (one of the few farm com-modities whose price has any relationship to parity) will give the dairy farmer an edge on the cash grain operation where prices are likely to fluctuate widely during a given marketing year. These are some of the economic reasons for the existence of the family dairy. They are not, however, the most important.

Perhaps Freud could get to the bottom of this business, but certainly there are irrational forces at work. What hold do huge Holstein cows with enormous bags and teats have on the dairy farmer's psyche? Is this black and white behemoth some sort of living and chewing security blanket? Is the daily routine of milk production some strong reaffirmation of moral principle? Is the hiss-hiss and pocketa-pocketa of the milking barn a re-turn to the womb with the splash of fluids, the heat of bodies, and the gurgling and discharging of many stomachs?

Whatever the real reason, men and women continue to work ridiculous hours in the family dairy industry. Its hold is strong. Some folks think more of their cows than they do their spouses. Perhaps some land-grant college will get government funds to study the psychology of the dairyman, but in the meantime, my advice is to stay clear of milk cows. There's something weird going on and you might get caught up in spite of yourself. Just think, twice a day for 365 days a year. Even heroin addicts get a day off now and then. Don't say I didn't warn you.

*Next week I'm going to
sit down and organize
things so I have time
to get my work done.*

Crazy Billy

Pioneering don't pay.

Andrew Carnegie

Crazy Billy
the Fantasy
Farmer

Almost every rural neighborhood in the country has a Crazy Billy. They may be philosophers, inventors, bookworms, or all three. Their fences are never fixed and their stock tends to drift around the neighborhood. Their crops are seldom planted on time and the rows are never straight. The farmstead itself is usually cluttered and unpainted. Change in operation occurs regularly. They may be into cattle one week and earthworms the next. Usually they have a long-suffering wife who holds down a paying job for the recurring financial fiascos and the monthly bills.

Crazy Billy farms 160 acres he purchased twenty years ago with an FmHA loan at 4 percent. In twenty more years it will be paid off. Billy is in love with rural life. It could be said he is addicted. Every morning he thanks the fates that he doesn't live in a smog-encrusted, crime-ridden urban area where he would have to drive in traffic to work at some boring job.

"What them people are is your basic trained rats. They get up, go to the car, drive through this maze to work. When the bell rings, they stop for coffee; the bell rings, they go back to work; the bell rings, they stop for lunch; the bell rings, they scurry back to work; another coffee break, a little work, and it's back in the car and back in the maze, all the rats pushin' on one another. On the way home they usually stop at a bar to have a few belts and then scurry home to where their wife and kids have been scurryin' through their mazes all day, school, shoppin', and so on, and are all pissed off from doin' all their particular bitin' and scratchin'. He takes his paper an' scurries to the TV an' watches what the rest of the trained rats have been doin' that day."

Billy is hardly a trained rat, although he suspects his neighbors of harboring some rat characteristics, what with planting corn simultaneously and other reprehensible behavior. If corn is supposed to be planted on May 10, Billy plants his on April 20 or June 15. If most folks use 115-day corn, Billy experiments with 85- or 120-day maturities. Even with constant experimentation, corn holds little romance for a farmer of Billy's stripe. He has grown mint, ginseng, organic turnips, artichokes, rape, sweet potatoes, pinto beans, and kohlrabi, all with mixed and usually unprofitable results. When his offbeat crops are good, he can find no market. When he scrounges up a buyer, he usually has no product. Billy has one entire grain bin full of ginseng roots; no animal on his farm will eat them. An ad in a farm magazine promised fantastic profits for ginseng raisers. A couple of letters and a check later and Billy had $5,000 worth of root stock and a contract guaranteeing him a tidy price for all the ginseng he could produce. Down in the fine print was a clause releasing the company from any obligation to purchase if the crop was not of sufficient quality, if the ginseng market deteriorated, if anyone's biorhythms were hostile on the proposed day of sale, or if the sun happened to rise in the east for two consecutive weeks. Billy read the fine print but was not dismayed.

"I figgered these folks would buy ginseng as fast as I could grow it. It's a miracle root, you know. It makes arthritis disappear and old men as randy as goats. If there's somethin' wrong with ya', ginseng'll fix 'er or know the reason why. With a root that'll do all that and more, who wouldn't buy it? Hell, folks could tell their doctors to go fly a kite. It didn't work out that way, a'course. I tried a few health food stores, but they wanted to take it on consignment, and most of them folks is pretty shifty lookin'. What we need is a George Wooshington Craver of ginseng. There's a good chance we can make shoe polish and synthetic grapefruit out of 'er an' I'm workin' on it. Mark my words, ginseng's the crop of the future. We'll see who laughs last around here."

Behind Billy's garage is a large galvanized shed that contains a shop that would make a NASA rocket technician salivate. Racks of tools line the walls, and drill presses, lathes, forges, welders, and cutting torches cover the floor. In one corner is an engine diagnostic center complete with grease rack and wheel-alignment machine. Most of this equipment was accumulated during two buying binges that coincided with Billy's home-auto-center idea and the search for a new machine to weed turnips.

In back of the shop is a pile of rusting turnip weeders that didn't work. In there somewhere is a homemade snow blower that didn't blow, a roll-over plow that didn't roll, an offset disc that no tractor in the neighborhood was potent enough to pull, a hay-bale accumulator that worked well until it got to the hay field, a controlled-environment farrowing crate that suffocated the only sow that used it, a baseball pitching machine with a skull fracture and four missing teeth to its credit, a mint crusher, a peanut harvester, a sweet potato grader and washer, not one, but two perpetual motion machines, a rain-maker, half of a homemade airplane (the other half was never recovered), two complete tank treads from Billy's military equipment phase, and an old freezer full of spare parts for a kohlrabi-sizing contraption that made everything the same size, roughly that of ping-pong balls.

Billy is not a fancier of livestock because they require feed and water on a semiregular basis. This has not prevented him from experimenting. His geese were eaten by coyotes, his dairy goats refused to give milk without adequate feed, his rabbits neglected to breed, his buffalo ran away, and his bantam chickens infest every nook and cranny of the farm. They lay tiny eggs in odd places and terrorize his dogs and cats by sneaking up on them, leaping on their heads, and driving sharp beaks into their skulls. The results are uniformly chaotic. Occasionally a banty rooster will attack Billy and his family from the rafters on the shop or barn, but he still likes them.

"We got all the eggs we can use and they ain't bad eatin' either, if we can catch the damn things. I never feed 'em, they just clean up around the yard and drink out of the pond or eat snow. Them banties is the best investment I ever made. Them buffalos was somethin' else. Don't let nobody ever sell you no buffalos. They're a pain in the ass is what they are."

Billy bought a bull and ten cows from a game farm in Indiana. Contented at first, they were a big attraction for Sunday sightseers in the neighborhood. The first spring every cow had a calf, and Billy had dollar signs dancing in his eyeballs.

"I give $10,000 fer my stock and I figgered them calves would be worth $500 anyhow. I'd have 'em paid for in two years, and then I could sit back and let the money roll in. The trouble was, they didn't respect a fence."

Buffalos don't acknowledge the existence of fences, let alone respect them. When the time came for fall roundup, Billy on his mule and his wife in the pickup began hazing the herd into a new railroad-tie corral. The old herd bull moved toward the catch pen, took a long whiff, turned, and hit the pickup going full bore.

"Stove the passenger door clean in is what he did, and if that weren't bad enough, he backed off and come at her from the rear. Took the tailgate off an' bashed in the whole left corner of the box. Then he went over an' worried a bunch of grass

with his horns. I figgered we'd just let 'em sorta' cool off, so I
moseyed ol' George, that's my main ridin' mule, over to the
pickup to see how Margie, that's my wife, was holdin' up, and
that damned buffalo come down on me like a damned ol'
freight train is what he did, an' he hit ol' George right up under the cinch an' rolled him and me over like a ten pin an' kept
right on goin'. Cleaned out twenty rods of fence, is what he
did. The rest of them buffalos went a roilin' out right after
him. They took the next twenty-odd fences they come to the
same way. Sure had some hot neighbors for a spell. All their
cattle got balled up together. Had a dickins of a time gettin'
them sorted back out. Meanwhile, George an' me had sorta
picked ourselves up an' was wanderin' back to the house fer
reserves. Marge, that's my wife, had already got home to
freshen up some. We got in the ol' family vehicle, that's the old
'58 Chev with three deuces, a three-quarter cam, an' a turbo I
sorta rigged up in my spare time. Well, we hit the road an'
followed the busted fences for about ten miles. I was hopin'
they'd stop when they got to the interstate; there's a damned
good fence runnin' beside 'er, but they didn't. They just took
a right turn and headed west, caused some fearful accidents is
what they did. There was lawyers sniffin' around here for a
couple of years after that wantin' to know who owned them
buffalos, but I wouldn't admit it, an' after I sicked ol' Rufus,
that's my meanest banty rooster, on a couple of 'em, they sorta
quit comin' and started writin' letters instead.

"I'll tell you, the comin' thing is earthworms. I got a shipment due in any day. A guy can make a livin' just raisin' a
garage full of 'em they say. I'll bet there ain't too many earthworms gonna bust through no fences and git lawyers down on
a fella. I sure wouldn't recommend buffalos for no kids' 4-H
project. They just won't stay put long enough fer a feller to
tame 'em down."

It might be assumed that Crazy Billy is the object of total

derision in his neighborhood. This is not the case. True, he is the butt of jokes and snide comments. Most folks find his farming methods appalling and may say something like "I'm getting as bad as Crazy Billy" if they're a day or two late getting corn planted. But underneath there is an undercurrent of warm feeling. Billy starts all the crazy projects they might attempt on their own if he weren't around. Lots of them have wondered about raising earthworms, but if Billy tries it out, they don't have to take the risk of being first. Even if Billy screws it up, they may be able to avoid his mistakes and turn one of his fiascos into a profitable venture.

After a trip to the state fair a few years ago, Billy came home and built a big round baler. He used some old grinder belting and the gears and wheels from a junker combine. The rest of the machine was an old Allis Chalmers Roto-Baler. Each bale took an average of four hours to make, since the machine needed constant adjustment. After a week of messing around, Billy gave up and consigned his baler to the disappointment heap behind the shop. The neighborhood watched as the hay project ground to a halt, leaving some twenty huge round bales strung across Billy's south hay meadow. When he tried to move one of the bales, it became apparent that he owned no machine capable of lifting them. He tried dragging them uphill with a chain, but the bales rolled off backwards, smashing trees and fences. Pulling downhill caused some interesting races between Billy and the bales as they broke loose and nearly mowed him down. After a couple of weeks and two or three failed inventions, he gave up. For two years the bales lay in the field while Billy made hay around them. Then one winter Billy's buffalo herd ran low on feed and he turned them into the big bales, since he couldn't move the hay to the buffalos. After the top two inches of each bale was eaten, the remaining hay was as green and fresh as the day it was put up. Billy's neighbors noted this phenomenon and the next summer the entire community switched over to big round balers made by a new company that had developed the early prototype Billy had attempted to copy. These machines produced bales that were easily handled by a new generation of movers, grinders, and wagons. If it hadn't been for Crazy Billy, the large round bale would have been several years later in its debut in the area and the neighborhood would have spent more long hours in the backbreaking labor of hauling and stacking small square bales that rotted when they were rained on and broke apart at the slightest excuse.

Even Billy's infamous buffalo project had its benefits for the community. The fence-busting characteristics and downright orneriness of the critters made such a lasting impression that when the highly touted Beefalo* cattle were offered for sale a few years ago at exorbitant prices, everyone in Billy's neck of the woods passed up the opportunity to get in on the ground floor. When Beefalo cattle failed to sustain their initial high value and took the same downward price spiral of many of the exotic cattle breeds, Billy's neighborhood was found lacking a single sucker. Their general reaction has been to praise their own foresight, but some public credit has gone to Billy's project for protecting their society from a boondoggle that could have collectively lost several thousand dollars.

Politics is not a great concern of Billy's community, especially politics as it relates to national and international affairs. Occasionally, a school board decision may galvanize some interest, or a county commissioner may raise the ire of his constituents by failing to have his roads properly maintained. Apa-

---

* A cross between cattle and buffalo, Beefalo were sold as being extremely hardy, easy calving, fast gaining, and able to convert roughage into savory grass-fat meat unlike conventional beef breeds that require a lengthy period of grain feeding to produce tasty steaks. All of this may be true of certain Beefalos, but to date they have not caught on, and the price of breeding stock has not been nearly as favorable as that of other exotics such as Simmental, Maine-Anjou, or Gelbvieh.

thy is the general rule, as it is in most of the country. Politicians are regarded only slightly more favorably than corn borers, and it is a rare individual who will admit he actually likes or supports a national political figure. Election time results in no bumper stickers, no yard signs, no telephone polling or any visible campaigning—that is, with the exception of Crazy Billy, who liked Adlai Stevenson and hated Nixon, adored Harold Stassen and distrusted John Kennedy, went wild over George Romney and ended up campaigning fervently for George Wallace, voted for Shirley Chisholm and George McGovern, covered his barn with Sargent Shriver posters, and gave his vote to Gerald Ford.

"I can't stomach those namby-pambies them easterners vote in, with all that bullroar about love and lower taxes. You'd think people wouldn't be so damned dumb as to swaller that crap every four years, but they do 'er. Purty soon them politician fellers are going to run a computer composite instead of a human being an' he's gonna win big. McGovern and Shirley Chisholm was my kind of folks. They screwed up so goddamned often ya' jist knew they was human. George was kind of a sissy mealy-mouth, talked kinda like that Boris Karkloff feller, must have bad dentures, but that Chisholm, she really smoked 'em. Ol' Goldwater's the one that got me all heated up. They asked him if he would nuke them Veet Cong, an' he said sure, why not, if they give us too much crap. They asked him what about this here Social Security, an' he said it was a crock, an' they jumped all over him both times. Now everybody wishes we'd have stood at home an' incinerated them Veets with a missile or two, or else just stood at home, and everybody agrees Social Security is a crock. That was 1964, fer Chrissakes. All them jokes about Barry being a backwards-lookin' feller an' he turns out to be damned farsighted is what he did!"

With so much apathy around, Billy just naturally does all the politicking anybody needs to do, thereby freeing other folks for important duties, like harvesting corn. His role is demanding, and it is little wonder that field work and fence mending often take a back seat. Whether he is inventing a new artichoke harvester or stumping for an obscure candidate, Billy makes no mistake about where his priorities lie.

"I guess I do pretty much what I feel like most of the time. What's the use of being a farmer if you have to rush yourself around to do certain things at certain times. It's a wonder some of my neighbors ain't had nervous breakdowns the way they carry on. Oh, they probably have more money that I do, but what's that compared to living the way ya want? Ain't that what money is supposed to do for ya'? Make yer time yer own? Besides, someday I may hit 'er lucky on some new contraption, git a patent on 'er, and make a mint is what I'll do. Me an' ol' Marge will be rollin' in diamonds, an' them other folks will suck in their cheeks an' plant corn. We'll be rich in spite of ourselves, an' even if we never git there, look at all the fun we've had."

Fun? Did the man say fun? Obviously deranged. Farming is a serious business where the weak are eliminated and the large efficient operation expands along carefully planned lines. As Mr. Butz said about agriculture before he moved on to general social commentary, "Adapt or die, resist and perish . . . agriculture is now big business. Too many people are trying to stay in agriculture that would do better someplace else." Obviously Mr. Butz never experienced the rare joy of owning a buffalo.

*I cheat my boys every
chance I get. I skin 'em
every time I can. I want
to make 'em sharp.*

William Rockefeller

*He that can have patience
can have what he will.*

Benjamin Franklin

Sherman
the Scalper

Sherman is indisputably sharp because he makes his living with his wits. Last year Sherman paid taxes on $75,000 but the government said he should have declared more income. They are still arguing about it. I suspect that, based on past performance, the IRS will not only lose the argument but be so humiliated that it will slink away and never come back. Sherman is a little on the mean side; it goes with his occupation.

In Sherman's neighborhood there are local livestock sales every day of the week but Sunday. He hits them all, arriving an hour before sale time in his four-year-old pickup, trailing a twenty-two-foot gooseneck stock trailer. He starts each work day by unloading what he has brought to sell. If the barn has a low volume and is dominated by odd-lot buyers, he may bring a few cows and calves, a dozen feeder pigs, and perhaps a bred sow or two. If the barn is a large-volume barn dominated by load-lot order buyers, he may bring thirty head of Hereford steers that he has put together over a period of several weeks while working the circuit.

While unloading his stock, Sherman will chat with the yard help, absorbing information on what livestock is already in or might come later. Then Sherman takes his morning constitutional through the yards. He notes each pen and mentally grades and prices its contents. This gives him the time and privacy to evaluate livestock before he enters the pressure atmosphere of the sale ring. He seldom bids more on a critter during the sale than he has decided on beforehand. Some buyers will get caught up in the emotion of a hot sale and bid more than they intended. They will become so involved in the competition to purchase that they will overlook defects and the real value of animals in the rush for ownership. Sherman is immune to such pressures.

If fat hogs and sows are first on the agenda, Sherman will look for wet sows, underweight fat hogs, piggy gilts, and cutting boars. If the packer buyers refuse to pay up for lame fat hogs, Sherman will own some of those. If top fat hogs are bringing 50 cents a pound, a lame one may be cut to 39 or 40 cents. Sherman will send them directly to the packer on a grade-and-yield basis. In most cases he will get full price. On a 230-pound fat hog he will make a profit of 10 cents a pound, or $23. If he buys ten gimpy fat hogs he will make $230, less trucking and occasional death loss, for a net of $190. Sherman purchases underweight fat hogs only if he believes the market is in an optimistic mood and will give him a good price in the thirty days it takes to bring a 180-pound hog up to 230 pounds. He must exercise great care in purchasing light hogs because the hog may have had pneumonia or scours as a youngster and may be a genuine poor doer and may take months or years to reach a desired weight. What Sherman is looking for is a healthy porker that the hog man has sent to town with some heavier hogs simply to fill out a truck load or to empty a pen needed for other pigs. An animal in this category, when freed of the competition of heavier, more aggressive hogs, will usually develop a good appetite and put on weight rapidly. Fifty pounds of gain will cost Sherman 25 cents a pound, or $12.50. If he buys a hog at a 7-cent discount, the cost is $77.40. After feed cost Sherman will have $89.90 invested in a 230-pound hog worth $115 at 50 cents a pound, or a net profit of $25.10 per head. Six head of light fat hogs will net Sherman around $200.

Profit in wet sows is somewhat more elusive. A downturn in the market can result in sizeable losses. Only if Sherman is firmly convinced that the market is sound will he venture into speculation in this area. Wet sows are those that have only recently had the pigs taken off. They are usually in thin flesh and sell at a 3-to-6-cents-a-pound discount. Sherman will buy wet sows only at a 6-cent or larger discount. Because sows do not convert feed as efficiently as younger animals, it will cost Sherman 30 cents a pound instead of 25 cents for the sows' gain. Thus, 90 pounds of added pork will cost $27. If good sows are selling for 42 cents and Sherman gets his for 36, the cost would be 350 x 36, or $126. By adding 90 pounds and bringing the sow up in grade, he will have an animal worth 440 x 42, or $184.80. Subtracting the feed cost of $27, Sherman will net $31.80 per head. If he buys five wet sows, his net profit will be $150.

Piggy gilts are fat hogs that have been bred long enough to show their condition. They will sell for a 10-cent discount from fat hogs. Sherman buys as many of these as he can lay his hands on. They are taken home and fed a light ration of alfalfa hay and grain so they do not appear overly fat. When the gilts look close to farrowing, he will put them in packages of six to eight head and run them back through the sale barn as bred gilts, where he receives about $200 per head, if the fat-hog market is good. Two months' feed bill will run about $36, and added to gilt cost of 230 x 40, or $92 will result in a profit of $72 per head. If Sherman buys ten piggy gilts, his profit for this day will run $720.

Cutting boars are small male hogs ranging from 180 to 240 pounds. They usually sell for a 15-cent discount from fat hogs and bring a 3-cent premium over big boars. Sherman takes his cutting boars from the sale barn to the veterinarian, who castrates them. He then takes them to the fattening pen where they are put in with the wet sows and light fat hogs. After thirty days the boars are healed sufficiently to be sold as fat hogs on a grade-and-yield basis. Thus, if the market holds, he will pay 35 x 200, or $70 each, for the boars. Vet expense, death loss, and feed will run another $16. On an $86 investment he will get a return of $122.50, for a profit of $36.50 per head. If Sherman gets eight cutting boars on this hypothetical sale day, his profit would be $292.

In two hours' time Sherman has toted up a potential profit of $1,552. Some of this money will be returned two days hence, while some may come in two months. But because he is constantly turning over his inventory, Sherman's profits roll in daily. But we are getting ahead of ourselves. Sherman is just getting warmed up.

Feeder pigs sell best in bunches of fifteen or more. This is because hog finishers like to feed groups that are already socially adjusted and will fatten at roughly the same rate. Sherman buys small bunches and singles. He specializes in navel ruptures and testicle hernias. Small bunches will cost five to ten dollars per head less than larger groups. Ruptures may sell for a dollar or two each. If he buys eight groups of six pigs, Sherman will sort out three groups of sixteen. If he buys at a six dollar discount, and by sizing and regrouping receives full price, he will net $264 by the next day when he sells them at another barn. The vet fixes ruptures by applying nitric acid to the stomach, creating scar tissue which draws the stomach up, removing the telltale bulge. Testicle hernias are fixed by removing the testicles and sewing the slipped digestive organs back in place. It will cost $5 to have an operation done, and death loss runs 20 percent, or abour 40 cents per head. Sherman must feed the pigs for three weeks before their injuries are healed. He will slip these pigs into his other groups and get full market value. Buying ten defective pigs will net Sherman around $300.

At this point in the sale the baby calves are brought in. Baby calves require special handling and Sherman's touch is sheer genius. At home in the freezer is a goodly supply of colostrum milk purchased from a local dairy. Each calf gets two quarts of this along with four raw eggs. Next they are started on goat's milk. Sherman's six nanny goats supply enough milk for twelve calves at a time. He spends his early mornings and late evenings fooling with his calves. The extra attention makes them more alert and consequently more likely to survive. Even though he specializes in buying calves that sell at a discount— those that are dirty and sickly looking—Sherman averages less than a 10 percent death loss. If a calf does not respond to the standard treatment, he is given a shot of whiskey, a shot of cortisone, a shot of vitamins A and B-12, and a diet pill and sold directly at the next sale before he has a chance to croak. All calves get a thorough bath and are sprayed with hair spray to give their coats a glossy sheen. Over the past ten years Sherman has averaged a twenty-five dollar profit on every calf he's handled. The purchase of five calves at this sale will net him $125 before the week is out. Baby calves are too likely to die to be very attractive long-term property.

The next item on the agenda is feeder cattle. Sherman usually gets a little shut eye during this part of the sale, when the competitive juices of his fellow bidders really start to flow. If the action gets too hectic, Sherman will go out to a bar and soothe his nerves with some cold ones before returning to the fracas. Sherman's chief objection to scalping feeder cattle is that they are expensive and the profit margin is small. There are several players in this part of the game, including the sale barn manager and several order buyers, a factor that limits opportunity. Sherman's particular favorites are large bull calves and heifers that have been bred too young. Bull calves about 600 pounds usually carry an 8-cent discount, and 550-pound bred heifers can carry a 25-cent discount. Sherman cuts the bulls and aborts the heifers. After a month's time he may put a package of either together and resell, or he may find the fat cattle market attractive and feed them out. His ten-year average on feeder cattle is $50 a head. If he buys six head, his profit will be $300. The reason Sherman has been able to maintain a $50 profit margin through bull and bear is that he is quite capable of sitting on his hands. Blessed with infinite patience, he will wait until his price will buy. If he does not succeed today, there is always tomorrow.

Sherman's own peculiar weakness is killer cows. When other people's wornout rejects come into the sale ring, he will actually move his stocking cap to the back of his head and shift his weight from one haunch to the other. Sherman is excited. He will duel other cow buyers with total ferocity. If they bid too high, he will run them up and drop out, sticking them with a loss. If they refuse to bid on a low-priced cow, Sherman will wink at the auctioneer and take possession after the sale for the starting-bid price. Fat, thin, cancer-eyed, lump-jawed, cadaverous, lame, or sick, Sherman buys them. Lump-jawed and cancer-eyed cows can be bought for five to ten cents a pound. When he gets forty head together, they go to a packing plant in Florida that pays full price for them. His thin old cows go to a packing plant in Omaha that pays a premium for thin cows. Old lean cow beef will take on a lot of water when made into lunch meat. Thin young cows go to his feedlot, where they receive a ration of ground ear corn for sixty days, then on to a packing plant that ships to a hamburger-patty fabricator that in turn supplies McDonalds. Fat cows and dairy breeds go to a packer in central Nebraska that cuts them up and ships the choice cuts to a national chain store warehouse, which peddles them to the consumer as U.S.D.A. choice beef, a blatant case of false advertising that the FTC has had no interest in to date. Sometimes one of the cows Sherman has consigned to the feedlot will surprise him with a calf. When this happens Sherman scrubs both cow and calf, gives them matching plastic eartags (leading the buyer to believe they came from a legitimate cattleman with a large herd), and trims the cow's tail, thus making her look a couple of years younger and adding to her value. The new family is then sold in a small sale barn where a single family may bring more than a bunch of twenty.

Over the years Sherman has averaged forty dollars a head on every cow he's touched. Cancer-eyes and lump-jaws have helped that average considerably, because he buys them for practically nothing. The cow business is not what it once was because of the loss of numbers out on the farm. In 1975 and 1976 Sherman could count on buying forty head a day even in a small barn. By 1978 Sherman felt fortunate to find ten head at a small barn and twenty-five at a big sale. On this hypothetical day he blows out the opposition and adds thirty head to his inventory. This comes to a cool $1,200 and makes his total earnings from one day's work a respectable $3,741.

Obviously not everyone can become a scalper. Brains and nerve in combination are a rare commodity in the general population, and Sherman possesses both in abundance. In addition, Sherman has a potential market in mind before he ever buys a critter. Knowledge of these sometimes obscure customers is what makes Sherman the very best at what he does. The last ingredient to successful scalping is a certain criminal bent that allows Sherman to sell a doctored-up sick calf with no twinge of conscience. Some folks would worry about the poor devil that might buy the calf and lose his money. In Sherman's world the buyer looks out for himself because no one else will.

In short, the livestock auction barn is Sherman's life and chief passion. Every day is a new game, and he has never come home with an empty trailer. If a fellow scalper drops a lemon on him in auction A, Sherman will drop a worse lemon on him by auction C. Farmer buyers are putty to Sherman because they are amateurs. He alone knows the real value of everything the barn has to offer on a given day. The price of cancer-eyed cows in Florida is not a major item on the financial page of the *New York Times*. Do not ever mess with Sherman one-on-one during a cow auction. If he cannot get you to overbid and hang yourself, he is quite capable of cleaning your plow with a tire iron. Packing houses no longer send buyers to Sherman's neck of the woods. The turnover in employees was fearsome.

The only way for a rookie to learn the business is to go to a barn and soak it up. With a limited amount of venture capital, feeder pigs and baby calves are the best items to learn on. Cows are for graduate students only and, if you've got a Sherman around, are probably not worth it even then.

*The Germans have
no sense of process.*

Tom Harwood

Why Aren't There More Irish Farmers?

Timothy Murphy, his wife, and eight boys own and operate nine hundred acres of marginal land some eight hundred feet above the elevation of the nearest running stream twenty miles away. The Murphy family is Catholic, well disciplined, and always looks a little tattered around the edges. The tattered look stems from the tradition of hand-me-down clothing and the utter impossibility of keeping eight healthy boys from ripping holes in newly mended overalls on a minute-by-minute basis. Tim has more labor available than any of his neighbors and he takes full advantage of the situation. His operation resembles nothing less than a hybrid cross of a Chinese commune and an Ozark hog farm. No road ditch within five miles of home goes unscathed in the summer when one of Tim's boys saddles up the faithful cow pony and herds twenty cows and calves up and down the road, bringing them home nights for water and rest and taking them out at dawn for another assault on free grass. Three older boys run a field chopper and mower all summer, sometimes straying twenty miles from home to cut a summer fallow field where the weeds got big. They clean the road sides as well as the railroad right of way. Every ounce of chopped thistle, firebush, or dry prairie hay goes into an ancient upright silo for winter feed. Last year the Murphy boys collected eight hundred tons of this free material. Interspersed in the silo are several hundred tons of wheatlage, oatlage, milo and corn stover, and barley straw. Murphys have sold no grain in twenty-five years. The corn crop is harvested in the ear and put in cribs.

The corn crib used to be a common sight on farms throughout the Midwest. With the advent of the picker-sheller, the more expensive process of shelling corn in the field, then drying and binning it on the farm or in town, phased the corn-picker out of existence. Ear corn stored in a crib would dry from exposure to the air and could be fed in the ear or shelled by a custom shelling crew and sold or fed. Anyone who has toiled on a shelling crew knows what it is to work. The cobs were used for fuel, efficient toilet paper, and poultry litter. Cornpickers lost more corn in the field than modern combines, but where cattle or hogs were put in the field following harvest, this corn was converted into cheap gain. More of the stalk was left standing after picking, catching snow, thereby increasing subsoil moisture. Modern gunslingers in four-wheel-drive tractors can hardly wait for the combine to finish harvesting before they are out there plowing the corn stalks under. This shortens the time required for spring planting and actually improves yields where soil organisms have been killed off by petrochemicals. Plow-jockeys with twelve hundred acres of corn to plant can't be expected to mess with cattle and hogs, and they don't. The lowly cornpicker lies in the tall weeds, forgotten and unmourned, on farms across the country. However, exceptions can be found. There are whole neighborhoods in southwest Iowa that never gave a picker-sheller a second look. Someday a fuzz-faced university researcher may wander down there to find out why those 160-acre farms are prospering in violation of all the computer models. If the student's brain is not overly befuddled by the advertising put out by the chemical and machinery firms that fund his work, he may find that drying charges can eat up 15 percent of a farm's profits and that corn cobs which are harvested along with the corn by the corn-picker can add 20 percent to a farm's available feed supply.

Tim Murphy hired a combine to harvest his corn one fall, but was less than pleased.

"The shelled corn that came out of the back end scattered all over the place. The hogs got most of it, but I still had volunteer corn blocking my irrigation rows the next summer. It took the kids a couple of days to cut it out with corn knives. The first blizzard piled snow up on my fences south of the corn field and broke them down. I'd never seen that before. It took the boys a couple of days to fix fence this spring. It cost me twenty cents a bushel to have it picked and another fifteen cents to have it dried in town. The boys had to haul it back out, and we got someone else's corn that was so dried and cracked it was half dust. The hogs wouldn't hardly eat it. Most of the boys around here use hybrid corn, and even if it weren't dried to a frazzle, the hogs don't like it as well. I went back to a cornpicker and I've never regretted it."

The man not only uses obsolete equipment, he doesn't plant hybrid corn. The whole country uses hybrid corn. If we didn't have hybrid corn, who'd buy all those pages of advertising in our farm magazines? Where would we get our free caps every spring? Hybrid corn out-yields other corn. It's easer to harvest. Who would deliberately not plant it? Blasphemy! Call the boys in the white coats!

Tim is not unmindful that his corn operation runs counter to prevailing wisdom.

"It's true we don't get the yields some of the farmers claim they get. Of course, it's a rare individual that tells the truth when it comes to his yield. I've seen a lot of 80-bushel corn standing in the field that made 150 bushel in the coffee shop after harvest. We get 115-bushel corn in the good years and 90 to 95 bushels when it's dry and hot. We rotate our ground so we don't usually have to use pesticides or commercial nitrogen. The boys haul a lot of manure in the spring, and we use some commercial soil conditioners. Sweet clover and alfalfa pay out as well as corn when we figure the inputs and the added livestock we can handle. We could probably raise hybrid corn the same way and get good results. The trouble with hybrid corn is that the seed companies charge too much for it and it's difficult to raise your own. My father started using this variety of open-pollinated corn over fifty years ago and we've saved the best every year for seed. It's adapted to this farm. A lot of hybrids are designed for use in states with climates more favorable to corn than this area. Most seed companies use virtually the same crosses year after year. This makes the crop susceptible to insects and disease. Our corn has a bigger, tougher stalk than most of the popular hybrids. We have less wind damage and less trouble with corn borer and rootworm. By raising our own seed we save about twenty dollars an acre. That's seven bushels of corn. We spend about ten dollars an acre on earthworms and commercial soil conditioners. Another two dollars probably goes for fuel to haul manure to the field. We save eighty dollars an acre on fertilizer, which equals 25 bushels of corn. We save about twenty dollars an acre in herbicide and pesticide costs. That's another 7 bushels. We'd have to raise 150-bushel corn every year to make up the difference, and most guys around here are lucky to average 125. The worst characteristic of hybrid corn raised the usual way is that it's actually inferior feed. You put my corn in one trough and your corn in another, and the hogs will eat mine first. The boys have run tests on rate of gain on the two kinds of corn, and the hogs on ours did a third of a pound better a day. They converted better too. That counts up when you raise as much livestock as we do."

Livestock is the name of Murphy's game, and his farm is overrun. Three windmills pump water into a series of ponds year-round. This livestock water cost him $37 last year, which was the cost of a new cylinder for one of the mills. Pond one waters his fat cattle and chickens, pond two takes care of his cow herd, and pond three takes care of his hogs.

Sows are farrowed year-round in old car bodies covered with haystacks. On top of each haystack is an old stock tank full of ear corn. Each morning one of the kids rides out in the pasture and throws out a little ear corn for the pigs. In the winter he may have to break ice in the pond so they can drink. Sows go into the cars on their own when it's time for them to farrow. No one helps them or messes with them in any way. When several bunches of pigs are ready to wean, the boys have a roundup. Since there are some five hundred sows running around out there, the roundup can be spectacular. The sows, pigs, and herd boars are driven into the barnyard and the pigs sorted off, castrated, and vaccinated. They are placed in one of a series of two-acre fattening pens. One of Tim's boys is on the road two or three times a week selling fat hogs. The past ten years Murphy has averaged seven pigs a litter, which is just below the national average. His fixed costs are negligible, however, and his profit picture is little short of astounding.

Fat cattle get a ration of silage, ground ear corn, and alfalfa hay. Tim buys cattle at the local sale barn almost every week. All cattle get the same ration, regardless of size or condition. The lot contains heiferettes, thin cows and bulls, choice steers and heifers, short Angus, and three-year-old grass steers coming in at a thousand pounds. The Murphys lost money only once during the cattle bust of 1974–77. A large measure of this was due to the abundant cheap feed produced on the farm. However, Tim is no slouch when it comes to buying cattle. Because he is not prejudiced against any particular kind of cattle, he can buy anything cheap, regardless of type. In contrast to feeders who can only see the Herefords and Black Whiteface coming through the sale ring (many of these feeders, incidentally, are no longer with us), Tim sees only price and condition.

"Sure, there were months we only got $1.50 for our corn marketed as fat cattle. Sometimes corn was $3.50 at the elevator. But we got a fair price for our roughage, and most of the cattle we fed were bought worth the money. Even though we feed odds and ends, we've topped the market on occasion. Big commercial feedlots don't like to buy cattle that aren't uniform. That's where the small feeder can slip in and capitalize on the opportunity. I can't compete with the big boys on large strings of choice Herefords. Nowadays, you have to take what they give you and run with it."

I naturally assumed that most, if not all, of Tim's boys, as they came of age, would be entering the business as full partners, but he surprised me.

"No way would I let them in here on that basis. I may want to sell out some year and take life easy. I couldn't do that with eight partners. Besides, they'd never really know what it's like to be on their own. Sure, I may help them out if I can, what father wouldn't? But if I haven't taught them how to make a living farming by the time they're out of high school, I sure wouldn't want them in my business. Each kid has to make his own way, try things out, see what works. They won't be happy otherwise. I'm not even sure there will be any farmers in that bunch. They've worked hard, and the money doctors and lawyers make looks easy to them. My youngest boy argues like a lawyer already. He comes up with new reasons every day why nine other people in the family should gather eggs instead of him. I'm proud of the boys, Mother did a good job. Nobody around here is going to force them into farming, although it won't take long for most of them to see the light. Ornery they are, but dumb they're not."

Tim's accomplishments have never brought him recognition. Tim's neighbors are not falling over themselves to emulate him. His profit picture would be impressive, if it were known, but since he buys secondhand cars and trucks and hasn't bought a new tractor in fifteen years, some folks think he's in real financial trouble. Practically no one would believe that he's made money on cattle for most of the past five years. Tim is not about to preach his gospel to his neighbors.

"Let the dummies find out for themselves. If they started farming like I do, they'd figure out a way to screw it up. The price of old car bodies would get so high I couldn't afford to buy them."

The only chronic cloud on Tim's horizon is the dearth of Irish farmers in the United States.

"I just can't figure out what happened to all those plowboys that shipped for America a hundred years ago. They had it rough in Ireland. The English stole everything that wasn't nailed down. Working for wages probably looked like a better proposition than starving on a farm while some landlord got rich. I have no way of knowing, but I would hope that if there were more Irishmen in agriculture, it would be a little less greedy and maybe a little more fun. Of course, I'm prejudiced, being sort of Irish myself."

*The land don't know who
owns it and don't much care.*

Larry the Lip

Larry the Lip: Wheeling and Dealing

Figures coming out of Washington indicate that Americans are losing their fear of debt. With pieces of Detroit junk running at eight thousand a copy and cheap houses costing sixty or seventy thousand, most consumers have found easy credit the only way to buy what is expected of them. Banks have helped out by pushing credit cards on anyone who would have them. Salespeople are trained to act insulted when customers pay cash for major purchases. About the only cash item in the consumer budget is food, a commodity hard to repossess after it is eaten.

Any High Plains farmer who lived through the depression has a deep-seated fear of debt. This fear has been instilled in their children, who plunge into debt with reckless abandon but feel guilty afterwards. The debt must be paid as rapidly as possible, for it is a black mark. One of the main goals of the game is to become debt free. It is the farmer's Nirvana. This is a difficult achievement, and in some cases, not even economically desirable. Some folks who overcame their inhibitions and bought land on credit have come out with their skins intact and with a sizeable chunk of change to boot. However, contrary to popular opinion, land investment has been an enormous burden on many farmers and has bankrupted a sizeable number. Taxes, interest, and principal payments go on inexorably through good crop years and bad. Families constrict their personal spending in order to pay off the land. Being "land poor" isn't any more pleasant than being any other kind of poor. Everyone hopes the land will be mortgage free someday. The day the torture stops and money can be spent on whims is the carrot that prods the donkey to continue the struggle. With the cost so dear, land becomes much more than a capital investment. A farm grows in importance until it constitutes a sizeable portion of the family's identity—it becomes both an economic albatross and a security blanket. The higher the cost of land in deprivation and worry, the more it is clung to and cherished. "The old home place may have turned us into paupers, but we love it." Larry the Lip suffers no such illusions.

The Lip got his nickname from his rapid-fire speech. His enthusiasms cause him to jump up and down and gesture wildly while he spews country small talk like a machine gun. If a good salesman could sell refrigerators to the Eskimos, Larry would have them begging for central air conditioning. It isn't that he lacks practice; everything he owns is for sale, including the wife and kids.

"It'd take about $6,000 a year to hire someone to do her work. I pay for her room an' board an' the dentist an' doctor bills an' her clothes. With hired help I'd get off cheap there. I'd have to hire some female companionship, but I ain't a heavy user so that'd run me around $400 a year. About $8,000 up front whip-out, an' she's all yours. Got a good set of teeth an' she ain't a bad doer. Keeps her shape on 1,500 calories a day. Kids I could let you have for a pittance, say $1,500 a crack. I can hire a kid by the week for eighty bucks, an' there ain't much more'n a week's kid work a year on most farms. Kids is too damned high priced to keep anymore. There's only so much paintin' an' weed cuttin' to do. I can't hardly use a kid till he's ten or so. Mine is four and six, so they're just about worthless. Sure, they're cute rascals, but I can't make no money on cute. If I want any kids in the future, I think I'll buy 'em full growed, let the other feller background 'em, an' I'll feed 'em on out."

Mostly what Larry has to sell is land. "We've moved about as often as there's been time to move. First we git a place, move onto 'er, and spruce it up, like. It ain't no different than what some city folks does with houses. I do the usual flashy stuff to the house, new kitchen cabinets an' new carpet. Then I trim up the trees, if there are any, an' crash an' burn all the junk. It'll take a couple weeks just gettin' the fences shaped up. If it's planting time I lay the fertilizer on double strength and git me a hell of a crop goin'. If it's fall, I buy me some hay an' stack it all around the yard like we raised a hell of a crop an' fill the granary to the top. That ain't a bad time of year to buy hay an' grain anyhow. I usually make money in a few months' time. Then I git on the horn to some money boys an' find out who's lookin'. If you realize who the buyers are, it don't take long to make a deal. Usually, I've got a couple places bought at once so we always got a home. I try to double my money. If I pay $200, I try to get $400, an' I usually git what I ask. Can't nobody in this whole country know what land is worth within $200 an acre anyhow. Inflation's runnin' wild an' munchkins is starvin' all over the world. They ain't makin' no more land, an' if folks don't buy now, it'll cost 'em ever'day they wait. If I buy a section for $200 and sell 'er for $400, I've got $128,000 to fiddle with. You do that two or three times a year, an' she adds up."

How does he find such succulent plums, ripe for the picking? No one can say Larry doesn't work for his money. "I shouldn't be tellin' you this 'cause it's sort of a trade secret, but you look like a close-mouthed guy. I sure would hate it if them old folks got the wrong idea. See, what I do is git me a county plat map. That's the one with all the land an' all the owners on it. If somebody dies, I check the map to see what they owned. Lots of times a widder will sell something just to pay estate taxes. First, I send her a condolence card with a ten-spot to show I ain't no cheapskate. Then I try to rent what I want to buy, sayin' how land's so expensive these days a man can't afford to buy any. Pretty soon she'll ask how expensive her place'd be if she wanted to sell it. I act kind of dumb an' say I wouldn't even want to guess an' that it'd scare me to think about it. Right away they're after me to put a price on 'er, so I shoot 'em a figure about thirty bucks an acre under what I want to pay, which gives me elbow room if they try an' jack me up. You'd be surprised how many of 'em want to sell right then an' there. If they chew on it a while, I may tell 'em a story about some lady we both know who sold out an' started wearin' nice clothes an' taking' cruises an' whatnot. I sure don't push hard. Just nudge 'em a little. Once in a while they git balky, an' that's when you cut your losses an' kiss ten bucks goodbye, 'cause when a woman gits stubborn you ain't gonna move 'er with dynamite. But, I git my share.

"Then I spend some time in the old-folks home. I got relatives in there, so I got a good excuse for bein' underfoot. I jaw around with them old guys an' it don't take long to find out who's ready to sell. Ain't many secrets in an old-folks home. By now people realize I'm always buyin' an' pay cash on the spot. I make it as easy as I kin. They don't like sellin' land in the first place. It's against their religion or something, so the less messin' around, the better they like it. Real estate agents just make 'em mad with all their sales contract talk an' the commissions. These folks ain't no dummies. They don't like giving nobody no 6 percent off the top. I save 'em the commission, so I buy for less. Why should the real estate guys make all the money?

"Another edge is that I'll slip 'em some cash money. They git a kick out of screwin' the government on the taxes and hidin' money from their heirs. It ain't too long after an ol' guy goes to an' old-folks home that the potential heirs come slitherin' out of the woodwork. Everybody knows old people don't last no time at all in them places, includin' the geezers them ownselves. It tickles 'em to death to stuff $40 or $50 thousand away in the closet that nobody knows about and ain't in no will. Just thinking about all them bald-buzzard heirs killin' one another off over all that cash puts 'em in a good mood for months. I suppose some of 'em even git a new lease on life.

"There's a time when I sell for cash, too. It improves my tax picture considerable. The boys that buy for cash, you don't want to know too much about. I think maybe some of 'em are sorta mean, if you catch my drift. They always have more cash money than they can justify from legitimate earnings, and I try an' help 'em out when I can. I usually end up managin' any farms they buy, an' that's 10 percent of the profits right off the top. I ain't never asked no favors of 'em, but if I was in a jam an' needed some nosey IRS dude flushed, they'd probably do it.

"Land auctions where the terms is cash is where I really git some beauts. Some days there's a whole bunch of buyers around with money in their pockets wantin' to buy. Other times it might be cold as hell or maybe people think the price will be high, so everybody stays home. That's when I step in an' lay out the ol' cold cash. If I can buy $150 under the market, it's pure profit. Most farmers maybe make one land deal in their whole life. The usual way of gittin' land is to have it gave to ya. If an ol' boy decides to buy somethin', price is not his main concern. That's his first mistake, but if he don't sell it for fifty years, it probably don't make no difference. If he's borrowing the money, his lender may give him some broad guidelines. He'll say, 'You could probably pay $700 an acre an' be all right; of course, it might only bring $500, and that would be really attractive, but if it brings $950 an acre, it wouldn't be out of line, the way land's been sellin' lately.' In other words, he don't know within $450 an acre what the place is worth an' don't care. He'll look at Farmer Brown an' either make 'em the loan or not. Price hasn't got a whole lot to do with it. Meanwhile, Farmer Brown is fallin' in love with this piece of land. He lets his imagination go thinkin' about all the great crops he's gonna raise an' how that particular piece of land is the only one in the world that'll suit him. It ain't no different than goin' head over heels about some girl. If the farm ate candy, he'd bring it some. You can see it comin' over 'em at a land auction sometimes. They git to breathin' hard an' their eyeballs git beady-lookin'. When they're that far gone, don't never bid against 'em. They go crazy. Price don't mean nothin' to 'em."

Has Larry the Lip ever fallen in love with a farm? "You betcha, I've done 'er an' it damn near ruined me. Once when I was in my cattle-baron phase, I fell in love with a ranch in Wyoming. It was crawlin' with deer an' antelope. Had a bunch of little streams runnin' through scrub pine. We had a little log ranch house with log corrals an' all. You couldn't find no prettier place nowhere. It wasn't a bad place to live either; the people out there are friendly, an' it's a real decent climate with open winters. Everything was hunky dory till we tried makin' a living on it. A thousand acres will run fifty cows. Fifty cows don't cut 'er, not when that's yer whole income. After I figured out what was happenin', I got me a chain saw an' logged 'er out. We sold enough timber off in two years to pay for the whole place. Then some of them pivot boys come along with some money, an' I up an' sold for a profit. That cured me for good, I hope. That ranch could have trapped me. If I'd have stayed in love, I'd never have took off all that beautiful timber. We'd still be pluggin' away, tryin' to make the payments, probably working winters in town, wearin' last year's undershorts.

"Land has a short-run value, what it should bring on the market compared with other land. It has a long-run value that has to do with the income it produces. Some guys buy at 5 percent return, others at 3 percent. If a farm will give the buyer $5,000 a year, it should be worth $100,000 to somebody. Five percent don't sound like much, but land has gone up every year lately. You add 12 percent inflation in value to your 5 cent and you git 17 percent. That ain't nothin' to sneeze at. It's when the crazy guys git to biddin' that land prices go out of whack. Here lately I've seen boys pay $3,500 an acre for land that would cash rent for $90. That's 2.5 percent. Can't nobody do that on borrowed money an' survive very long. You'd have to find a sucker an' sell out before it killed ya. It don't make sense, especially when there's land bringing $250 that'll cash rent for $40. That's 16 percent interest an' you got yer land inflation to boot."

I once asked Larry if he ever planned to settle down. "Don't you think it would be nice to have your own place that you weren't figuring to sell next week? I'd think your family would get tired of all the moving."

"Well, now that you mention it, they have been crybabying here lately. It'll git worse as the kids grow older an' pick up friends. The wife sees where we have the money to stay put for a while, an' I ain't gittin' any younger. (Larry is twenty-eight.) If I could find a place half as pretty as that ranch in Wyoming, I'd be sorely tempted. It's a free country out there an' we could afford a bigger place this time around. It'd be nice to step out on your front porch an' pot a deer if you needed freezer meat. I just might do it. Some of that land has got coal under it, you know. If a man could sneak up on a dab in the coal company's backyard, he could put the screws to 'em on mineral rights, an' after they got done strippin' her out, you could put in a hell of a trout farm in all the ponds. Then you could. . . ."

You get the picture. Larry is as hooked on wheeling and dealing as most folks are on their own particular ruts. Larry wins at the land game because he does not carry the emotional baggage that hinders most of the other players. There aren't many Larrys around, which is probably just as well. However, we shouldn't dismiss his theology completely, for there are little nuggets of wisdom strewn through it that any serious player of the farming game cannot afford to ignore. Purchasing an entrancing piece of land may give us an emotional high, but the piper must be paid, and frequently the romance turns very sour indeed. A farm with high earning power relative to price will often times be the wallflower of the ball. It will not have sex appeal nor will it keep us awake nights. If we put our dreams of a seductive farm aside, grit our teeth, and buy the sturdy economy spread, we will no doubt find all sorts of hidden endearing qualities, not the least of which is a certain inability to bankrupt.

The
Farming
Game

All the smart boys say cattle are going to go down the toilet. That's why I've been buying every calf I can lay my hands on.

Milton Tupper

The Smart Boys

Smart Boys is a term of mysterious origin. It refers to commodity brokers, spokesmen for meat packers, grain, and chemical companies, presidents of various farm organizations, and the agricultural "experts" employed by the government, colleges, and universities. Every farm publication staffs its share of smart boys who churn out articles by the bushel dealing with everything from the probable price of hogs next year to the mysteries of soybean herbicide.

What most of the smart boys have in common is the erroneous belief that farmers should be more rational than their fellow men. They worship agriculture as the last bastion of capitalism, the deliverer from world famine, the only bright spot in our sick balance-of-payments picture, and the most productive segment of the economy, in contrast to those bad guys in blue collars who get big wages for taking coffee breaks. They hold farmers (as opposed to the farming industry) in ill-concealed contempt for failing to follow the rational models they construct to forecast the future. No machinery company successfully predicted either the explosion of farmer buying that followed the high grain prices of 1974–75 or the dramatic slowdown which hit in late 1977. In 1974 the companies were caught with their pants down and did not have enough machinery to meet the demand. In 1977 they had machinery running out of their ears. Fertilizer companies deliberately restricted supplies in 1974–75 in a familiar ploy to raise prices. The resident smart boys had prepared charts showing fertilizer consumption would continue to rise even at $70 a ton more because farmers would make money on the higher yields produced with fertilizer. For a year there were allotments, black markets, fertilizer trucks darting into farmsteads in the middle of the night, and the companies made lots of money. They built up their plant capacity to meet the expected demand that was slow in materializing. Somehow farmers lost interest in heavy fertilization during the enforced scarcity. In spite of the proliferation of graphs and articles in farm publications showing that heavy fertilization generates more profits, fertilizer use failed to reach projections. The romance was gone from fertilizer. It is difficult to program a computer to construct a demand projection based on anything so fickle as a love affair. It is no wonder the machinery and fertilizer market specialists have become wary of predicting farmer buying patterns.

There is, however, one class of smart boys that thrives on farmer irrationality. Nobody hates a stable market more than a commodity broker with a mortgage. If you want to see a smile on his face, let pork bellies go straight up, with shorts scrambling to cover and anxious buyers ringing his phone off the hook. Or let broilers plunge to life-of-the-contract lows, with sellers unloading their heavy artillery and longs digging foxholes. Erratic markets multiply commissions, buy new Porsches, and make alimony a whole lot easier. Have soybeans tick by at 6.74¼, 6.74½, 6.74¼, and the brokers may start a telephone chess game just to look busy. To avoid stagnation it is necessary to develop stories.

The bugs have gone ape in Iowa. Even if they spray, the corn crop is going to be down 30 percent and we all know what that means.

There may be bugs in Iowa; there usually are. They may be

eating corn like crazy, or they may just be thinking about it, doing practice laps around the fields, getting in shape for the big crunch. The smart boys don't really care. They pick up the phone, dial the customers, whisper conspiratorily, "The bugs are going ape in Iowa, and you know what that means," and the buy orders pile up. Corn goes 3.64, 3.65½, 3.66, 3.66¾, some shorts will get nervous and buy back a little. The ticker goes 3.67, 3.67½, 3.68. Some farmers out in the boonies will call up to check their hedges sold at 3.52 on the advice of the broker who predicted a bumper harvest. The government crop report said so. If the farmer's boonie is in Iowa, he may be puzzled about all the bug stories.

"Where are all these bugs supposed to be?"

"All over Iowa, they claim the crop is going to be down 30 percent."

"Well, I ain't seen no bugs, and nobody else has either."

"Well, you live in just a small part of Iowa. Maybe you fellows are lucky this year."

"No, I checked it out. I've got cousins all over the state and none of 'em have seen no damned bugs."

"I wouldn't worry about it. We still haven't changed our fundamental position that the market is overbought and will soon recognize that the near-term supply is burdensome. I have a note here that says you owe $1,200 in margin money, so we'll need a check by Monday."

"Don't you think I should get out?"

"Sure, you might even consider buying a contract or two, this bug news has got three to five points left in it."

"Are you telling me I should buy?"

"Not necessarily, if this news is as exaggerated as you say, corn is bound to slide to support level, which we have at 3.32 on the chart. Your sell at 3.52 should hold up long term."

"These margin calls are killing me. I'm afraid to see my banker again; he's getting nervous, says the Russians are going to buy a wad in the next couple of months."

"No kidding? Where'd he hear that?"

"He says his broker told him."

Commodity markets are, of course, not restricted to farmers. The supposedly staid process whereby a wheat farmer sells his crop for future delivery at a set price and General Mills buys wheat, ensuring a supply for its flour- and cereal-processing divisions, has deteriorated into a national crap game. A filling station owner from Long Island might buy thousands of pounds of pork bellies every year. When the stock market bores the socks off investors, you can see the old ladies in tennis shoes loading up on iced broilers because there's an awful disease brought in by communist parakeets that's going to kill all the chickens. Some folks get rich. Others owe $1,200 a month for the rest of their lives, all of which is great fun. What bothers nonspeculating farmers is that their well-planned business decisions of selling, say, December wheat at $4.50 a bushel, may get blown to smithereens by some crazies from Boston who heard a smart-boy rumor. Margin calls can eat up enormous amounts of capital. The impetus of a rumor may die, leaving the market permanently higher than it would have been. Because a farmer selling short can usually make money only if the market goes down substantially, (this is because of the difference in basis between his local market and the delivery terminal), a rumor-inspired upswing can ruin his hedge.

University professors have devoted a lot of ink in recent years attempting to instruct farmers in the intricacies of hedging on the futures market. Most of these writers know enough to be dangerous. Their oversimplified prescriptions, if followed religiously, would quickly bankrupt the average farmer. Agricultural periodicals present these maunderings as if they were holy writ, in spite of their woeful inadequacies. Little mention is made of the heavy market participation of huge agribusiness firms. Continental Grain can blow the market up and down all by itself, in spite of the one-hundred-fifty-contract limit. The ineffectiveness of this limit was demonstrated by the Hunt family during the great sugar bull market of 1975–76 and the silver boom and bust of 1979–80. Armour and Wilson may have their own reasons for flushing a pork belly contract ten points. Suffice it to say, if they want it to happen, it will. This game, with giants bashing into each other, crunching the little folks between them like insects, is what the university smart boys are recommending to "progressive" farmers as a new marketing tool. The futures market may well make them wealthy, but if farmers make their trading decisions on information from the smart boys, they may progress right out of farming.

You may say that no one holds a gun on the farmer forcing him to follow smart-boy advice. Enormous pressures to do so, however, are applied by agricultural lenders, who go to conventions where these same experts are featured as guest speakers. To the lender, hedging is portrayed as an excellent method of minimizing risk. Loan a farmer $50,000 to produce a soybean crop, have him sell the crop on the December futures for $50,000, and the loan principal is covered by insurance. Beautiful, except no one mentions the yellow-eyed wolves out there watching the individual sales pile up on the short side of the contract. Let some bugs go ape in Iowa and the wolves will chase the boonie shorts from Pisgah to Creston. There was a well-publicized case a few years back about a farmer who hedged his hogs at the cost of four quarters of land that had been in the family for over a century. He has been forgotten in the rush for progress. No doubt the smart boys will claim a substantial number of new victims before they rediscover a "new" marketing tool, like forward contracting at the local elevator, as a definitive answer to fluctuating commodity prices.

Not all university smart boys concentrate on helping farmers with marketing decisions. Quite a few of them are scientists devoting careers to the improvement of crop yields and the development of superior livestock breeds. Most of the popular varieties of hybrid corn were developed by these men in white coats. Seed-corn companies have profited handsomely from this research while the farmers who were taxed to support it got buried under the growing mountains of surplus corn and had the privilege of buying the chemicals and fertilizers necessary to keep the fragile plants alive. Bushels per acre and production costs per bushel rose as the inflation-adjusted price per bushel plummeted. The scientists received acclaim for increasing gross farm income and feeding the world. Some of them were given nice raises and more graduate students, others went to work for the seed companies at double their old salaries. Missouri 17, a popular parent strain developed at the University of Missouri, found its way into a whole generation of commercial hybrids sold by J.C. Robinson, Trojan, and Northrup King, among others. They were not assessed royalties nor were they charged development fees. Profits rolled in, and the white coats received public applause. Nobody seemed to notice that the genetic base of corn production was being depleted and that insects and diseases were gaining ground on the high-yielding favorites. The maize dwarf mosaic virus hit Ohio in 1964. In 1968 came phyllosticta leaf blight, and in 1970, eyespot leaf blight and the T-male sterile cytoplasma disease, popularly called southern corn blight. The latter cut corn production substantially in the South and the Midwest and resulted in shortages and higher prices for blight-resistant seed-corn varieties the following spring.

Why was so much blight-susceptible corn grown? Dan McCurry writing in the *New Land Review* gives the answer.

They saw the chance to reduce their costs by eliminating much of the field labor involved in seed corn production. Cross-pollination in a corn field is eased due to the separation on the plant, of the tassel carrying the male pollen and the silks which each lead to a potential kernel embryo. Fertilization occurs when the pollen lands on a silk and extends a tube through the silk to fertilize the embryo kernel. Pollination control, for cross-breeding purposes, means removing tassels from a seed-bearing parent to prevent self-pollination. This is the mid-July hand-labor task performed by thousands of midwestern high school students and migrant workers. Row-by-row, thousands of acres were annually detasseled, thus allowing wind pollination from selected male parents planted nearby.

This hand labor seemed unnecessary after the development of a male sterile cytoplasm during the mid-1950s. The tassels were made genetically infertile by crossing the female line with this source of male sterility. Then the male line was genetically restored to the degree that the female parent produced a seed from which a pollen-producing plant came the following year.

Despite the genetic vulnerability of major seed-corn varieties demonstrated by the 1970 experience, USDA-sponsored university and private seed-corn research has continued to concentrate on high yields and genetic uniformity, at the expense of research into insect and disease resistance. One day the bugs will stop taking laps and wipe out a big chunk of the nation's genetically weak corn crop. Much finger pointing will result. The EPA will get blamed for banning all the good pesticides. The universities will blame the government for not providing sufficient research funds. The seed-corn companies will blame the farmers for wanting to buy high-yielding varieties. Farmers will initiate a lot of class action lawsuits against everyone in sight. Food prices will go through the roof, and the Ralph Nader of that time will lecture housewives on the cooking of gravel as a tasty meat substitute.

Not satisfied with populating American farmland with vulnerable high-yielding corn hybrids that require expensive machinery, fertilizers, and chemicals to produce, university and seed-corn company smart boys have launched a campaign to repeat the process in the underdeveloped world. Sixty-five percent of Argentina's corn crop comes from De Kalb seed. Architects of the "green revolution" are working like bandits to produce varieties of rice and wheat that will outyield older established versions grown in Africa and India. Some of them get Nobel prizes. The specter of global crop failure and accompanying famine does not dent their enthusiasm one whit. If new research adds twenty bushels an acre to rice production, the white coats can make a reservation on the next plane to Stockholm.

Ponder what would have resulted from stagnation of corn yields at 1929 levels, roughly one-third of today's. There would be little grain available for export, although the high prices might make up in value what the grain lacked in volume. Foreign farmers, no longer burdened with chronic competition from cheap American grain, would have been encouraged to increase their own production, making urban crowding in the Third World less of a problem than it has become. Higher grain prices would have kept small American farmers competitive and allowed them to stay on the farm. The public would have paid much more for food, but the very real costs of forced urbanization, decaying city school systems, rotten core areas, increased expenditure for police, fire, and insurance protection, geometric increments in welfare spending and welfare-caused family disintegration would have been largely avoided. When the time comes to fully thank the plant geneticist smart boys for all their contributions, will mere words suffice?

One of the few examples of tax-supported agricultural research that has attracted significant public criticism is the U.S. Meat Animal Research Center at Clay Center, Nebraska. Beginning in 1966 with 35,000 acres of land, a budget of $3,750,000, and 75 employees, the center now skimps by on

$6,000,000 per year,* employs 38 scientists and 277 support personnel, and plans to add 300 staff members in the near future. Initially, local people were delighted at the expanded employment opportunities the research center would provide. Real estate values in the small towns surrounding the center have skyrocketed in the past few years. Businesses have prospered and farm families have welcomed the off-farm income. When stories of inefficiency and waste filtered out, most looked at the new houses going up around them and shrugged, their attitude being quite common among folks experiencing government largess for the first time. What was more disturbing was the direction of research: swine breeds especially suited to confinement and thereby to corporate hog farming; confinement sheep husbandry with similar implications; and heavy use of artificial insemination in cattle, a practice more likely to be followed by well-heeled drugstore cowboys than by dirt farmers with small herds. No one questioned the need for meat production research, but the type of experiment popular with the white coats seemed more likely to put small farmers out of business than to provide any long-term benefits. A new agricultural engineering facility opened in 1978 that conducts research on the problems of housing, waste management, and environmental stress commonly found in highly capitalized, investor-owned livestock-confined set-ups. Were the climate of ag research to change and national emphasis to be placed on the small family farm, the white coats at the Meat Animal Research Center would no doubt develop experiments more adaptable to the undercapitalized operator.

It is not only the Center's research that undercuts the small operator. The sheer amount of tax-subsidized meat production of the facility has also become a hot issue. Approximately 2.4 million pounds of beef, 374,000 pounds of pork, and 160,900

---

*This excludes annual budget income from the sale of livestock and wool, which ranges between two and three million dollars.

pounds of lamb and mutton flow into the open market every year in direct competition with farmer-produced animals. The National Farmers Organization in particular has been incensed over this practice but has been unable to halt it. Producers of foundation stock in the cattle and sheep industry must also compete with the tax-subsidized breeding animals sold by the Center. Such sales have had an adverse impact on purebred breeders, particularly in surrounding areas of southcentral Nebraska and northcentral Kansas.

You may wonder why this place isn't picketed or bombed by a bunch of angry farmers. The answer lies in the pervasiveness of the idea that technological progress improves farm income, and after all, there are all those new houses going up.

Whenever there is a public policy debate that has the slightest implications for agriculture, a dozen smart boys employed by the various farm organizations show up armed with graphs and charts ready to do battle for the farmer. Usually their testimony results in a general free-for-all in which the Farmers Union and the National Farmers Organization (NFO) spokesmen end up throwing bricks at the Farm Bureau representative, who has just advocated a program diametrically opposed to theirs. The Farm Bureau almost always wins its points because it represents the largest constituency, hires more persuasive people, and is backed by the boys with the most cash, but there is always a chance the other guys will get really irritated someday, and the poor Farm Bureau smart boy will end up riding a rail. To put it mildly, these organizations don't get along. Once in a blue moon they will agree on something. In 1973 when Nixon left the price freeze on meat, they screamed in unison, but such action is rare.

The credo of the Farm Bureau is simply to get the government the hell out of farming. Since most farmers see the government as an enemy, this is a popular philosophy. There are, of course, certain qualifications to this simple theology. Present government research is applauded, as are administration efforts to market commodities abroad. Tax-financed water projects, no matter what their environmental or economic implications, are usually supported. Bureau of Reclamation irrigation endeavors are good, but limiting land holdings to 160 acres within those projects is bad. Legislation favorable to labor interests is always bad. Tax laws benefiting the nonfarm investor are good. If nothing else, the Farm Bureau has been consistent over the years. A speech made in 1981 will sound identical to one made in 1944.

The brick throwers complain that the Farm Bureau is more interested in selling insurance and fertilizer than in protecting the family farm. They claim most Farm Bureau members aren't farmers at all but businessmen who purport to speak for farmers. They point to Bureau positions over the years that would seem to support monopolistic dominance of agriculture and they cry conspiracy. The fact remains that the Farm Bureau's philosophy appeals to a significant number of farmers. Local chapters generally do an excellent job of placing their views before local and state government officials. National Farm Bureau lobbyists have more clout than the small organizations and will, no doubt, continue to exercise it.

The National Farmers Union consistently backs legislation favorable to cooperatives and small farmers. Critics maintain the two are mutually exclusive. Organized in Texas at the turn of the century, Farmers Union sought to band farm commodity sales into cooperative marketing groups. As organizers worked north, co-op gas stations, elevators, creameries, livestock marketing associations, and grocery stores sprang up. By 1928 there were 250 cooperative grain elevators in Nebraska alone. Farm Bureau spokesmen were also advocating cooperative endeavors but were pushing improved production techniques at the same time. Farmers Union remained suspicious of university research and sought government help in limiting production. The cooperative movement suffered reverses. Members sometimes lacked the ability to run their own affairs, and hired co-op managers gained a well-deserved reputation for thievery and book juggling. Eventually, cooperatives became Frankensteins, controlling large segments of fertilizer production and grain marketing and operating with blatant disregard for the interests of a majority of their members. They operate with impunity to the antitrust laws and are financed with unlimited funds by the Bank for Cooperatives, which sells bonds on the national money market. Profits, which used to be distributed to members, are now generally plowed back into expanded facilities and wage increases for the hired help. The small local co-op that bought cream and eggs and sold groceries, shoes, and barbed wire, and paid dividends like clockwork became an exception. It was replaced by branch offices of the "giant co-op in the sky" and, while ostensibly controlled by local member boards, actually carried out policies decided by empire builders somewhere upstairs.

Most co-ops still pay small cash dividends. However, the primary rebate instrument is an infinite supply of stock certificates, paper with limited liquidity and dubious value. Co-op smart boys are adept at public relations. Local officers are kept pliable with subsidized trips to Hawaii, and farmer-members are sold on becoming part of a large enterprise like a hog-slaughtering plant or a large grain-export facility. The big co-ops and the privately owned agribusiness giants have mutual interests in increased production and capital-intensive farming practices. Farmland Industry's fertilizer division is unlikely to be even mildly interested in organic farming.

Farmers Union has, nonetheless, consistently supported government policies that favor smaller operations. No doubt this creates some confusion at times when position statements are worked out. Being a part of the "great co-op in the sky" has its attractions for the small farmer, and the co-op knows that without some members out there in the boonies, it might have to borrow high-priced money like anyone else. This diverse empire seems destined to run along, building huge elevator complexes, while its farmer members sit back and feel rich. It's an interesting compromise.

If all the mean, angry, radical farmers in the United States were put in one room, over half of them would probably belong to the National Farmers Organization, headquartered in Corning, Iowa. You may recall that at times NFO members have shot their own hogs or dumped milk on the ground. These demonstrations were designed to publicize "holding actions." Holding actions were called to boost prices toward a predetermined "cost of production plus a reasonable profit." The idea of farmers holding their products until granted a certain price is not new. In its formative years, the Farmers Union flirted seriously with the idea before abandoning the practice as unworkable. Faithful members held back production while their neighbors sold like crazy on any market upturn. Eventually economic pressures forced the holders to sell grain or overly fat animals for what the market would pay. The Farmers Union shifted gears and went into the elevator business before widespread disillusionment destroyed the organization. The NFO, beginning in 1955, concentrated its energies on signing contracts with meat packers, milk distributors, and grain companies. The companies were supposed to pay a certain price for the product. In return, the NFO pledged delivery of so many hogs, cattle, and so on, per week. In an unusual twist, not only were dues-paying members assessed selling charges, but buyers were asked to pay for the privilege. Processors were slow to sign contracts, and holding actions, calf shoots, and milk dumping resulted. If the price went up two cents during a holding action, the NFO took the credit. If the price went down, nobody remembered; or if they did, they attributed the slide to the Rockefeller-Farm Bureau Conspiracy. Eventually a few packing plants entered into NFO contracts. Organizers, out beating the bushes for members, preached that the new day was at hand. Collective bargaining for farmers was a reality. Dues poured in. Meanwhile, the packing plants found they had been forced into a very good situation. The NFO was out there lining up a regular supply of cattle of guaranteed quality, and all the packer had to do was pledge payment of, say, three cents a pound over the going price. These bonus pledges were frequently ignored, of course, but fiction sells at a premium, and the NFO had plenty of fiction to sell. Oren Lee Staley, the permanent head and driving force, stumped the country preaching collective bargaining to an increasingly receptive audience. Meanwhile, his cronies were appointed to important positions within the organization, particularly as trustees of the various accounts that handled the money from all products sold through NFO's marketing operations. These trustees held effective financial control over the administrative side of the organization by determining which part of the marketing fees would be handed over and which shaky marketing projects would be subsidized. Staley's chronic mismanagement of funds and failure to win meaningful price increases became forbidden discussion topics. Malcontents were shouted down or branded as agents of the Rockefeller-Farm Bureau Conspiracy. Farmers were put under intense pressure to sign up. Local business men were blackmailed into buying tickets for NFO dinners and expensive ads in NFO publications. The price for noncompliance was a farmer boycott. Public criticism of Staley or NFO practices became tantamount to calling the Pope an atheist.

Actually, it's hard to argue with the economic theories of the NFO. Yes, Virginia, the Chase Manhattan Bank does sit on the boards of some big food chains and they do have interest in egg and broiler production. Monopolistic corporations and cooperatives have come to dominate our food-distribution system. There can be no doubt that small farmers, in particular, have suffered from this trend. It is also unlikely that these institutions arrived at their present level of economic power purely by accident. However, I have my doubts whether an eastern banker woke up one morning and said to his wife, "Today I'm going to get into broiler production, ruin all the small growers, send them packing to town where they'll have to build new houses, which we'll finance, and make all kinds of money." Maybe the bankers are that smart, but if they are, they ought to fire those people who talked them into making those funny loans to Upper Ubangiland. Rather than railing at some well-organized conspiracy, the NFO might be better served if it gave credit where credit is due. Institutional stupidity is a pervasive force in this country and, when banded together by interlocking directorates, can become awesome, not only in its economic power but in its lack of foresight and incredible social bungling. As long as evil-genius conspiracy buffs are out in the bushes, the NFO will continue to sell them snake oil. More farmers will sign contracts and their prices, with certain exceptions, will continue to be about what anyone else gets. Few basic questions will be asked about the way farmers conduct their business because NFO says there is no such thing as a surplus, only market manipulation. Every farm problem from drought to low goat-milk prices has one solution: NFO sponsored collective bargaining.

To be fair, the NFO has been remarkably successful in a number of marketing efforts. Dairy programs in Wisconsin, Minnesota, and Ohio have gained a respectable market share, are self-supporting, and contribute substantial revenue to the home office.

The responsibility for the achievement of the dairy program in these areas lies largely with the administrative skill of the local NFO officers and with the nature of the product (it comes out daily in fairly predictable amounts, which can then be guaranteed to the processor). Other marketing gains have occurred in Montana feeder cattle, fat-lamb forward sales to packers in western states, and with hog production in Iowa, southern Minnesota, and portions of Illinois and Missouri. These specific programs demonstrate that NFO marketing can result in immediate price benefits to producers.

In geographical areas with sparse membership, similar attempts have resulted in unfavorable contract terms and have run up administrative deficits which then had to be made up from the revenues from more successful programs elsewhere. It is not unusual for a load of milk to be shipped from Minnesota halfway across the country to meet a contract shortfall. Ohio and Michigan, with large, modern NFO-owned grain-handling facilities, may have to make up a contract delinquency in Nebraska, where loading operations may consist of a rail siding wrangled from the local co-op, a six-inch auger, and a tractor tire, and take four days to complete. Despite such difficulties, isolated individual NFO members continue to pay dues in the hope that someday the marketing channels regularly used by the organization elsewhere will be made available.

A blunder that plagued the NFO for several years was the financial difficulty of the Iowa Grain Trust. Farmers sued NFO for overdue grain payments, and the Securities and Exchange Commission contended that the trust was bankrupt. NFO's shoe-box record keeping was shown to be woefully deficient, and the practice of capitalizing delinquent dues was called into legal question. Staley survived the extended battle with the SEC, but dissidents within the organization began to sharpen their axes. In all probability Staley would have lost his job in the early days of the NFO if he had chosen to play by Queensbury rules. Staley's rumored method of silencing convention opposition was to have the appropriate membership cards disappear, thereby turning potential rivals into official nonpersons. Then there were Staley's cronies heading the various marketing trusts who could threaten to cut off funding for local collection points. If all else failed, dissidents would be shouted down as secret agents of the Rockefeller-Farm Bureau conspiracy.

Troubles with the Iowa Grain Trust finally galvanized Staley's opponents into concerted action. Staley's friends, choosing between personal loyalty and civil war, eased him out. Devon Woodland, Staley's handpicked successor, has shown himself to be less of an evangelist and a much superior manager. He has moved cautiously in replacing the cronies Staley left behind, perhaps because many of these fellows still sit as guardians of the organization's purse strings. Eventually, these people will be gone, replaced by the well-scrubbed, rational types that inhabit Farmland Industry offices. Meanwhile, record keeping has gone from slipshod to computerized, strong programs have been given the benign help of a consistent national policy, and the weaker programs have received some steady, if belated, attention.

The NFO may never reach its stated organizing goal of 30 percent of this country's farm production. At the present time a best guess would be that it is marketing around $825 million worth of farm products annually for an administrative cost of about $850,000 (down from over $1 million under Staley). NFO handles roughly 7 percent of the fluid milk, 2 to 3 percent of the hogs, and less than 1 percent of the grain and cattle sold nationwide. Recent efforts to organize corporate hog factories may give a major boost to the hog numbers marketed through NFO, but such moves hardly support the notion that NFO is the ultimate savior of the small family farm. As average farm size continues to grow, it would surprise no one to see the National Farmers Organization, champion of the independent operator, getting into bed with those Rockefeller-Farm Bureau types who run our nation's largest farms. After all, that's where the production and potential marketing fees are concentrated.

Whatever happens in the future, NFO politics should continue to be fascinating.

There are many farm organizations besides the three mentioned here. The National Cattlemen's Association, the National Meat Board, the National Pork Council, and various trade groups representing cotton, milk, wheat, tobacco, and others collect dues, conduct lobbying efforts, and hold conventions. The big three are more universal in scope and carry more clout than the others. If an Arab camel breeder bought some farmland in the United States and began doing business, the Farm Bureau would try to sign him up and sell him some cheap insurance, the Farmers Union would try to get him to buy camel feed at their co-op elevator, and the NFO would attempt to persuade him to market his young camels through collective bargaining. American Agriculture would persuade him not to raise any camels at all or, at the very least, to buy the mandatory fifty-seven embroidered AAM patches to sew on his burnous.

The American Agriculture Movement was born in the fall of 1977 in eastern Colorado. Depressed wheat prices in particular and low grain prices in general sparked the organization's efforts. They pledged not to buy any new machinery after December 14, 1977, sell any grain, or plant crops in the spring of 1978 unless legislation was passed making it illegal to sell farm commodities at less than 100 percent parity.* They held tractor caravans throughout the country to publicize the farmers' problems. What city folks saw was a bunch of supposedly broke businessmen driving down the street in $50,000 tractors. Critics said the striking farmers would have gotten more sympathy if they had hauled out the old A John Deeres and driven them to town. If the message failed to reach the average consumer, machinery companies and small-town businessmen

---

* *Parity* is defined as the amount those commodities were worth relative to manufactured goods before World War I.

took notice. Trade hadn't been too brisk before the strike, and if these guys were serious, a lot of folks were going to be locking their doors. Donations poured in from implement dealers anxious to please. "We Support the Farm Strike" signs appeared in store windows across the High Plains. Farm magazines at first laughed at the strike, then did an about-face when subscription cancellations came pouring in. Farm organizations tried to ignore the strike. AAM turned the heat on, urging members to stop paying dues to these "decrepit" organizations that had failed to win high prices for farmers. Only the Farm Bureau held out, and it has suffered a significant, if temporary, loss of farmer membership as a result. Farmers Union backed the strike. NFO tried to get out front and siphon new members into collective bargaining. NFO does not release membership figures, but it's probably a good bet that they gained at least as many members as the Farm Bureau lost during the strike.

Most insurgent groups identify enemies upon which they heap abuse for creating the conditions being protested. In the case of the AAM, the enemy became (who else?) David Rockefeller and his brainchild, the Trilateral Commission. The official explanation that the Trilateral Commission was simply a group of international scholars, businessmen, and government officials who were interested in promoting world peace and understanding did not wash with the AAM. They saw it as a comspiracy by world-government advocates to supplant national politics with some vague brand of international socialism. AAM speakers and publications traced members of the commission to their positions of responsibility in business and government, where they presumably were working to implement Rockefeller's personal vision of where mankind should be headed. AAM spokesmen contended that the only beneficiaries of low commodity prices for American farmers were the major banks who had loaned huge sums of money to less-developed countries. Some of these countries, the theory went, could only repay the loans if their agricultural products were purchased by the United States and its allies at the expense of American commodities. Other Third World borrowers that had spent their loan money on imported energy from Rockefeller-controlled oil companies and on industrial technology from Rockefeller-controlled factories might need cheap food to keep their populations happy and productive.

People who hate federal income taxes regaled AAM meetings with charts and graphs linking taxes to the long-range purposes of the Trilateral Commission. Anti-gun-control advocates and groups opposed to abortion took their shots at the Rockefellers. Gradually, the elements of several protest movements were blended into the philosophy of the AAM.

After criticizing existing farm organizations for a lack of reponsiveness to local membership, AAM was at first reluctant to elect officers or form a formal organization. It took six months for this democratic urge to die away, and AAM is in the process of erecting a bureaucracy. As we all know, the strike did not succeed. After all, there are three million farmers out there, most of them buying or selling whenever they damn well please. But what about next time? By 1985 there may be only 250,000 farmers. A real strike would be much easier to organize, and the effects. . . .

Whether AAM will go the route of the big three is an open question. Signs point to yes, but the jury is still out. There are some empire builders at work. They can't seem to forget how easy it was to extort money from the local hardware store. Some of them got to like Washington, D.C., and they may well end up as paid lobbyists. When you start seeing American Agriculture insurance and the American Agriculture grain elevators, you'll know the party is really over.

Every large bureaucracy, government or private, is certain that it conducts its affairs in the only way they can be conducted.

Milton Friedman

Inefficiency should not be subsidized in agriculture or any other segment of our economy.

Ezra Taft Benson

In the formulation of board policies and bank procedures, consideration shall be given to the peculiar needs of farmers engaged in highly specialized, high risk enterprises and the special credit needs of young farmers to the extent the bank/ or association has financial resources and staff capabilities to do so on a sound and constructive basis.

Rule 4165 of the Regulations for Banks and Associations of the Farm Credit System of the Farm Credit Administration

The Irrational World of Farm Finance

Since colonial days, American farmers have borrowed money to plant their crops. Early southern planters borrowed against future production of cotton, rice, indigo, and tobacco, not only for legitimate business expenses, but to maintain Scarlett O'Hara life-styles that were deemed more important than profits. George Washington followed common practice in developing a debtor-creditor relationship with English tobacco merchants. They sent out fine crystal, furniture, fashionable clothes, and machinery, the costs of which were subtracted from George's next year's crop. George grew tired of the arrangement and complained of his chronic debts. He had married some stock in the Bank of England, however, and not long after he became president, he was buying pieces of new banks that had sprung up under his administration. Obviously, George figured if he couldn't beat 'em, he'd join 'em.

Farm credit expanded rapidly in the South, which had more capital-intensive agriculture than the Northeast and the Middle West. Slaves were expensive, as was the constant depletion of soil that regularly caused new land to be purchased and cleared. Southerners gradually acquired a tomorrow-is-another-day philosophy of debt. Their northern contemporaries grew to hate banks with a passion. As states were carved from the upper Middle West, laws were passed giving bankers the legal status of horse thieves and Indians. Antibank forces gained an unexpected ally when Andrew Jackson, himself a plantation owner, destroyed the Second Bank of the United States and with it twenty years of progress toward a national money market. From 1840 to World War I, farm credit was a chaotic system composed of merchant lenders, eastern and British money, railroad-financed land purchases, and government homestead procedures. With the establishment of the Federal Reserve System in 1913 and the Federal Land Bank in 1915, a semblance of order was created. The war brought high prices for commodities and encouraged even higher land prices. On the Great Plains, where growing conditions were hazardous at best, farmland values reached levels not seen again until the early 1970s. Booming land prices were fueled by the speculative bent of zillions of small rural banks that had sprung up, by the august Federal Land Bank, and by cash-heavy insurance companies. The 1920s brought lower commodity prices, and farmers, banks, and insurance companies began an epidemic of bankruptcies that did not falter until World War II.

In 1935 the Resettlement Administration was set up to allow the neediest farmers to get a new start toward self-support. Only farmers on relief were eligible for help, and they often lacked the will power to benefit from government aid. A few small packages of land were redistributed, but because the modest goal of the program was to create a subsistence food base for farmers on relief and not to set up viable small-farming units, few lasting results were achieved. The RA was absorbed by the Farm Security Administration in 1937. Under Rexford G. Tugwell, the FSA broke new ground in attempts to get land into the hands of sharecroppers.

J. J. Richardson worked as a county supervisor in southeastern Missouri under the Resettlement Administration, the Farm Security Administration, and later the Farmers Home Administration. He was present at the creation.

"Our first money from the Farm Security Administration allowed us to buy enough land to pick the best farmers from the hundreds of applications we had. As it happened, we put six white and two black families on the farms, which ranged from 60 to 80 acres. They were supposed to keep the land for five years. Some of those folks are still living on their farms. The loans were for forty years at 3 percent interest. Most of them paid off early, as I recall. It was a very successful program. Some farmers bought machinery together and we'd loan them the money.

"Back then we encouraged people to milk a family cow and raise a garden. Most of them weren't used to much, but they were good managers and they made it. Local people were all for the program. We got some static from the newspapers and some politicians. They said it was socialism. I thought we did a lot of good and could have done more, but we never had enough money to help everyone that was qualified. We sure sweated over some of those applications. It was a big responsibility."

Walter Harkey still lives on the land he purchased from the Farm Security Administration.

"I've added some land since then, of course, but if it hadn't been for that program, I'd never have got hold of any. Chester McMillan, Jimmy O. Lee, and I are the only ones around Hornersville that got started then and are still living on our farms. I don't see how anybody starting out now could make a go of it. Land is just too high priced. How are you going to pay for $2,000-an-acre land? Some of the land that went into the program was purchased from Security Farms, which was a bunch of rich guys in Chicago. I was president of the co-op that handled the purchase and distribution. We put forty-one families on the land. Most of them left in the '50s. Pretty soon it will be one big farm."

Tugwell's pet project was at La Forge, Missouri, where 6,700 acres were divided among one hundred families. The Farm Security Administration erected prefab houses on the land, and dignitaries toured the project bathed in media attention. The American Farm Bureau was incensed at land distribution in general and at the La Forge experiment in particular. They viewed it as a giant step toward godless communism. The political heat increased. In the South the program's land sales to blacks was anathema. Funding became difficult when the Roosevelt Administration shifted its attention to international affairs. The program was allowed to die, and, with the evolution of the Farmers Home Administration in 1946, less radical measures were adopted.

FmHA opened its doors for business staffed by dedicated employees who had worked hard during the Depression keeping farmers on the land. Its mandate was less sweeping than that of the Farm Security Administration, but policy direction was similar. Tenant farmers occasionally qualified for farm-ownership loans (funding was always limited), but the majority of FmHA loans were and are now made in the form of short-term farm-operating loans. As the carry-over New Deal enthusiasm was diluted by bureaucratic procedure, and consummate paper pushers were elevated to administrative positions within the FmHA, Catch-22 provisions were implemented which, if religiously followed by a local loan officer, would eliminate any applicant from consideration for farm ownership loans. To be eligible, farmers cannot obtain credit elsewhere. If a man is so destitute that even the neighborhood loan shark will not take a chance on him, he must also prove to the county advisory committee (sometimes made up of big operators with little interest in the problems of their competition) and the county superviser (who hopes a good rating by his county committee will help him get a promotion) that he is a competent operator. If by some strange quirk of fate he passes the first two stipulations, the farm he proposes to purchase must be of sufficient size to "constitute an efficient farm-management unit." This provision effectively eliminates almost everyone who has passed the first two examinations because, even if he finds a farm to buy that qualifies, he must prove he can generate enough income to pay for it. If he picks an 80-acre farm he could afford, he is denied the loan because the farm is too small. If he selects a 320-acre farm, he is denied because he cannot show proof that he can make the payments. It must be said that there are areas in the country, Missouri in particular, where red tape is ignored and a genuine attempt is made to aid small farmers. In general, however, the FmHA has become a professional bureaucrat's delight. Mountains of government forms are shifted from one office to another. New forms are printed to cover every conceivable situation, and new paper pushers are hired to deal with them. More paper means more jobs, more jobs mean more supervisory positions and the correspondent increase in fief-building and desk-size competition. I knew a fellow in Nebraska who applied for a farm-ownership loan to increase the size of his operation from 400 acres to 560 acres. He passed all the tests and was approved only two and a half years later. By then the farm had been bought and sold three times and was in the hands of an absentee investor who had installed a center-pivot irrigation system.

In the Deep South, small black farmers in particular have had a difficult time extracting any sort of funding from FmHA. In some cases, former Farm Security Administration projects have been left to twist in the wind, and attrition rates among original participants may run as high as 98 percent. Bill Harrison of the Southern Rural Policy Conference, headquartered in Montgomery, Alabama, has had an opportunity to study credit problems suffered by small farmers in the South.

"I doubt whether 20 percent of these guys are still full-time farmers. They raise some vegetables to sell in town, maybe some tobacco for a cash crop. Some of them raise a few turkeys or feeder pigs. Most of them would like to expand, maybe get more livestock, but if the FmHA don't go, they're done. Banks and the PCA are out of the question for them. The FmHA says they're too small, too inefficient, but they won't loan them money to get efficient. If somethin' doesn't change, we're going to lose a lot of these guys that really want to stay on the land."

As we have said, FmHA spends most of its time processing farm-operating loans. This can become a real power trip for some local officials. They hold the capability to destroy the survival of most of the farm families that come to them. They often use this power to personally degrade and abuse their customers. A county supervisor in southcentral Nebraska has a standard speech that he gives to new applicants.

"Let's see what we can do here to straighten out this mess you've made of your farm. I see you're milking cows and far-rowing hogs. Nobody ever made a dime doing that. We'll have you sell your cows and sows. That'll let you concentrate on farming, although nobody ever made a dime doing that either. We'll have to see where you're wasting money (If you weren't wasting money, why would you be here?) and put you on a budget. Your wife will have to prepare more food at home, or maybe we'll have her get a job. Can she do anything? I mean, would anybody hire her? Then we'll have to see what your clothing budget is every year. Maybe you spend too much on underwear or something. We'll find out. I'm not saying we can do anything, of course. This operation is pretty far gone to salvage. Have you thought of selling out? It might be best for everyone concerned. You could make a living working for someone else. We're short of funds now anyway, and even if you qualified, which I doubt, it would take a year or so to get any money. See this (indicates a large stack of applications on his desk)? That's everyone that's ahead of you, but if you still want to apply (sigh), I guess I can put your application (sneer) before the board."

This guy has ingeniously developed a method of further reducing applications by scheduling office hours only one day a week. He then takes his accumulated sick leave or attends conferences only on that one day. No one has figured out how he has escaped promotion. Surely such devotion to duty deserves recognition. Whatever path his career takes, he has no fear that he will be removed. When farmer and congressional complaints about his performance were funneled into the regional office, form letters were promptly issued informing addressees (including congressmen) that the FmHA was doing a good job, thank you, and that if anybody needed money, he should go to his county supervisor who would fix him up.

Whatever its shortcomings, the FmHA has done some good over the years. There are conscientious loan officers out there in the trenches making loans to people in spite of FmHA regulations. If you are in the game and have such a man working your area, count your blessings. If you have serious intentions of entering the game and plan to make use of FmHA money at some point, it would be well to get a neighborhood reading on the local government money vendor before choosing a permanent home. It is possible to do business without such help, but unforeseen disasters can put your back to the wall, and there may be no alternative.

The Federal Land Bank is a money co-op. It sells bonds on the money market and makes long-term loans for land acquisition and improvement. Since 1971 it can also make loans for the purchase of houses in towns of 2,500 population or less.

Member borrowers buy stock in the Federal Land Bank, which is paid off in installments along with the interest and land principal. Each borrower has one vote, which is used primarily to elect the oversight committee of each local Land Bank Association. This committee officially hires the managers and dictates policy. In practice the local manager does business pretty much as he wants. In many areas the Land Bank has become a private club loaning money to a select few, who are then able to buy land any time they want. Committee members can veto loan applications, but usually the Land Bank manager will "check out" a potential borrower with the committee member from the area on an informal basis.

MANAGER: Hello, Hiram?

HIRAM: Yeah.

MANAGER: This is Winslow over at the Land Bank. How are the crops looking out your way?

HIRAM: We could use some rain, but they're coming along.

MANAGER: That's fine. Say, Hiram. I had a guy here the other day that wants to buy the old Geezer place, name of Billy Jo Dust. You know him?

HIRAM: Yeah, he's a neighbor, young kid. I didn't know old-lady Geezer would sell. I've tried to get that place bought several times.

MANAGER: Oh, you're interested in that farm?

HIRAM: Well, I could be if the price was right. How much is she asking?

MANAGER: I think he said $250 an acre.

HIRAM: Is that all? Pretty reasonable.

MANAGER: What do you know about this Billy Jo Dust? Is he reliable?

HIRAM: I hear he pays his bills, as far as that goes. He don't have much in the way of machinery. I heard his cows were pretty old. I think some of them died last winter.

MANAGER: You don't think he's too good a risk then?

HIRAM: I've seen better.

MANAGER: I'm just nosing around. Sometimes application forms don't tell the whole story. This Dust, for example, has got a real good cash flow and his net worth is high for a young guy.

HIRAM: Well, he ain't above stretching the truth.

MANAGER: Oh, he lies a lot, does he?

HIRAM: I wouldn't say a lot, but the facts don't always jibe, if you catch my drift.

MANAGER: I certainly appreciate your advice, Hiram. We'll take another look at this thing. Better to find out these things now, than have a loan go sour.

HIRAM: Any time. Say, do you suppose I could get the money to buy that Geezer place if this Dust thing falls through?

MANAGER: I would sure think so, Hiram. You get her talked into $250 an acre and you've made yourself a buy. That place joins you, doesn't it?

HIRAM: Yeah, it would fit right in.

MANAGER: Well, you get her bought, and we'll find you the money. How's that?

HIRAM: That's all right. We'll see you at the next board meeting. And thanks.

MANAGER: That's what we're here for.

Every year the Federal Intermediate Credit Banks publish figures showing their lending has increased by so many zillion dollars and wait for applause. What the statistics don't reveal is that in its purely agricultural sector the Federal Land Bank is loaning more to fewer people, in spite of regulations stipulating that such lending agencies take a flyer on young farmers who would not ordinarily qualify. It has become comfortable to service existing customers or the man who walks through the door wanting three or four million to swing a deal.

This is not to say there are not some Federal Land Banks out there with even-handed lending policies. I have known a few loan officers who gritted their teeth and made loans they knew were shaky to farmers who had experienced adversity. Since the Land Bank is usually the only game in town for long-term mortgage money, it will take a little time for the pilgrim to discover whether or not it is a closed club in his area. If it is, he maybe should think about settling somewhere else.

Production Credit Associations usually operate in conjunction with the Federal Land Bank. PCAs finance farm operations, livestock facilities, and other short- and intermediate-term credit needs. This too is a money co-op, and everything previously stated about the Land Bank applies to PCAs in spades. An average loan from the PCA will run $70,000 and up. Most farmers don't even gross $70,000. If your local lawyer has a Subchapter S Corporation out there raising turkeys like crazy to help his tax situation, there's a good chance he borrowed the money from the PCA. Hog-confinement facilities, gigantic beef feedlots, corporate broiler operations, and commercial fish hatcheries have been heavy users of PCA credit in recent years. Critics maintain the PCA has done more than any other financial institution, public or private, to ruin the profitability of agriculture for the majority of those engaged.

This is beginning to sound grim, you say? It is. However, you and your friends can always start your own money co-op and borrow funds from the Federal Credit Bank. Some wise-acre slipped a provision into the Farm Credit Act of 1971, which allows folks who are not being "adequately serviced" by existing agencies to put up a little money and borrow ten times that amount from the bond pool the big boys dip into. The catch is that being "adequately serviced" means different things to different folks. The burden of proof is on you. If you raise enough hell, you might get your money or, at the very least, force the local Land Bank or PCA to set some new members into the club. Nobody said this game was easy.

Banks, like women, are not
supposed to take the initiative.
They consider proposals and
say yes or no.

Bray Hammond

All a banker has to know
about anybody is whether
they're good for it. If a man is
in the habit of paying his
bills, he'll probably pay back
the loan. Property statements
and mortgages aren't worth
the paper they're written on.

B. J. Tupper

Do not be fooled by the soft carpet, the indirect lighting, the monstrous time-and-temperature sign outside, or the quiet music playing in the background. This is not a world of conscientious caretakers of the public trust. Rather, it is a den of inveterate gamblers, most of whom are building card houses on tiny amounts of equity that would scare the wits out of a stone Las Vegas junkie. Ever since Alexander Hamilton created the nation's money supply and concomitant banking system out of Federal indebtedness (a move so brilliant in its inception and so brazen in its execution that most folks still don't understand it), bankers have shown no reluctance to take a plunge now and then. Nicholas Biddle, president of the ill-fated Second Bank of the United States (the direct ancestor of our present Federal Reserve System), set out with the money he didn't have to corner the world cotton market. It was not the last time the commodity market would break a fairly bright guy. The stock boom of the twenties was fueled by bank loans. In 1929 bankers were given the highest windows to jump from. Bert Lance was disowned by the banking establishment for kiting checks, making loans to himself, borrowing on the loans, and buying a banking empire, all at the same time. Actually, compared to a lot of bankers, ol' Bert was pretty respectable. For ten thousand down you can buy a bank with a book value of one million dollars and deposits of ten million. You can't buy much of a house for ten thousand any more. Banks are more fun than houses anyhow. With a bank you can smoke cigars, buy a really nice house, make weighty statements on the economy, and have folks drooling all over your Italian loafers. Who else can generate a couple of zillion dollars a day in new money, up the interest rate two percentage points, and sit back and blame the government for causing inflation, and be believed? Bankers have a lot of fun, but it's not all roses. Saving and Loans keep horning into their territory with electronic checking and free glad bags, and credit unions are becoming real pests with their cheap interest and reasonable service charges. Then there're examiners from everywhere wanting to know how many loans they've made to Negroes and women lately.

The small-town independent banker probably comes closest to fitting the common close-fisted stereotype. There's one in western Nebraska that won't loan money on cars, says they're too risky, and another that has 5 percent of his deposits loaned out and the rest socked away in government bonds. Most of these characters like to know how you're going to pay the money back before they give you any.

Small-town bankers like to know who they are doing business with. Most of the good ones keep family trees in their heads. If a customer is a second cousin of Crazy Billy, his application gets a mental caution flag. Ike Grable as a fourth cousin twice removed would open the vault. When in doubt, bankers furtively reach under the desk and feel their pulses. If the vibes are good, they make the loan. When signs are bad, they become instantly short of funds. Good bankers want their funds loaned out, and sometimes that's a much harder job than they let on. Show these guys a decent proposal and some security, and they'll usually go for it. Don't tie up their money very long, pay it back on time or maybe a little sooner, and in no time you will have found yourself a valuable business partner.

My prejudices, freely admitted, favor the small-town (less than 800 population) banker who has loaned up to between 60 and 85 percent of his deposits (this shows that he works at his profession) and who has some real knowledge of agriculture. I do not like chain banks, banks owned by multibank holding companies, or branch banks. These folks are more likely to be interested in short-term profits and in empire building than in the long-term interests of their communities. The holding-company board of directors may decide tomorrow that turkey ranches are good and that milk cows are bad. Maybe some smart boy just gave a lecture on declining milk prices at a convention. Overnight the dairy farmers will start having farm sales, and turkey flocks will proliferate like gerbils. Or, as has happened on more than one occasion, a city bank with several rural subsidiaries will decide all farm lending is a bad risk this year and will put all their eggs into the condominium market uptown. Farmers out in the boonies, faced with lots full of half-finished cattle and no credit to buy feed, will start dumping assets, depressing the market, and fulfilling the smart-boy prophesy. If the condominium market goes sour and the bank is stuck with a few million dollars in shaky loans, it can always scrounge up ten thousand someplace and make a down payment on a cash-heavy rural bank that can be robbed for its assets while the condominium market is getting well. These large banking organizations all have cloning laboratories behind the vault where ex-gestapo scientists whip out branch managers by the gross. They come equipped with bright little smiles and ten-word vocabularies with terms like "highly leveraged," "attractive cash-flow," "positive attitude," and "customer feedback." Programmed to make the big loan, they panic over a note for five thousand to a man who pays his bills and is worth two hundred thousand. Have a fast-buck operator show up with a three-hundred-dollar suit, two cents in his pocket, a "positive attitude," and a scheme employing two million bucks to build a mechanized goat nursery, and the clones will try to loan him an extra million. In contrast, the competent country bank operator lives in one town all his life. His customers are his friends and he likes to see people prosper. If he is a prudent businessman, profits will be adequate and he can indulge in charitable lending from time to time for the greater community good. He is seldom thanked for such behavior. Folks are too envious of his position. However, secure in the knowledge of a job well done, a banker can ignore such slights.

If you can find a good country bank similar to what I have described, marry it on the spot. You may never get another opportunity. The freedom to operate without the restraints of government or co-op red tape can mean money in your pocket, not to mention the increased peace of mind you will experience from dealing with an expert seat-of-the-pants operator with a sense of history. Clones and government bureaucrats have no memory beyond their last mistake, nor are they competent to run your business. If they were, they would be on their own instead of on a payroll.

It is barely possible to farm without credit, but it's a very tough road full of jam tomorrow and never today and tends to make folks grab loose nickels and stuff them under the bed. Find a good, solid country bank, give it all your checking and saving accounts. Put a solid enterprise together, say a small farrowing operation, out of your own capital. Then go in and borrow the money to feed out some pigs. This should account for about 30 percent of the fat hogs' eventual worth and will be paid back in four months' time. The banker will be able to see that his loan is adequately secured and that you can pay him back from the sale of the hogs. This is a good way to begin a banking relationship. Later, if you decide you need to buy some cows that might take three years to pay off, he will be more inclined to trust you with the money. Do not lie to him, cheat him, or abuse him in any way. It is much easier to go through divorce and find a new wife than it is to leave a good bank and find another. Unless you are independently wealthy, credit of some kind is essential for any self-sustaining farm enterprise. Where available, the small country bank will fill this need completely, and you will not have to ensnarl yourself in red tape or grovel at the clubhouse door to get your money. Whatever your circumstances, stay away from the clone banks if at all possible. Heap bad medicine: make grass short, and buffalo go down highway. Besides, it's hard to have a positive attitude when they tell you it's time to put up the sale bills.

A small country bank cannot supply your long-term mortgage money. If there is a need for money to buy a farm and there are problems with the local Federal Land Bank, you have two alternatives. The most popular choice is to finance the sale with the seller. Usually, he will want 29 percent down but occasionally can be persuaded to take from 10 to 20 percent if the price is right. If the seller is quite elderly, he may want a contract of only ten years. This is a dangerous game to play, because a farm will not usually pay out in ten years. At today's land prices, it might not pay out in a hundred years. A private land contract for twenty years at 10.5 percent interest, with the provision that it can be paid off after five years is worth more money per acre than a ten-year contract at 11 percent with no early pay-back provision. This pay-back provision is a safety valve. If you run into adversity and need to borrow on the equity portion of your farm, the lender will probably want a first mortgage. He cannot obtain this unless you pay off the contract holder. A ten-year contract with no early pay-back provision locks your assets up where you can't play with them. Your only recourse in such a case is to get an FmHA loan (they'll take a second mortgage) if possible, or sell the farm and its ten-year contract to someone else and go buy another.

The other alternative is to borrow money from an insurance company. They usually loan money at rates competitive with the Land Bank. As a rule, they aren't bad people to deal with, although they spend a lot of your money on expensive lawyers who examine titles and abstracts until the ink wears off. They also like to make big loans—$100,000 and up. Some of them have million-dollar minimums. They require healthy down payments—up to 50 percent—which, if you have the 50 percent, is no problem.

Recent fluctuations in interest rates have made insurance companies gunshy about committing funds for extended periods at fixed rates. Some have provisions calling for interest rate renegotiation every three years. Others are making five-year "bullet" loans, which involve making interest payments only for four years and paying the entire principle back in the fifth year. This is a hairy method of financing for most operators but is of some value to speculators who are planning to resell their property within five years.

For most people, the land contract is the most attractive way to buy a farm, and, because it has tax advantages, is still the most popular way to sell. The byword is to watch the interest rate. There is no reason to pay over the going rate for CDs, and an extra 1 percent can make 50 dollars-an-acre difference in land cost over the life of the contract and bankrupt the buyer in the process. Most sellers are greedy folk who would rather have ten dollars more an acre now than 1 percent more interest later. Use this greed to your advantage when writing the contract.

Whatever credit source you choose, it would be well to remember that more farmers have suffered from overborrowing their repayment capabilities than the reverse. When faced with a backbreaking job, it is easy to borrow money to buy a new machine that will do the work in a flash and help the tax situation in the process. These impulse purchases bankrupt farmers every year. If you feel your check writing hand getting itchy, give it a cold shower. Tomorrow the work may be done, or you may find a neighbor who will lend the equipment, or the work will become unimportant after all. Once you make an expensive purchase, it will sit around drawing interest long after any work is done. As Sherman the Scalper says, "Patience ain't a very flashy virtue, but it sure pays better than most of 'em."

Stick with me, kid, and
you'll be wearing horseturds
big as diamonds.

Willie Nelson

How to Beat
the System

During the past thirty years, countless, ambitious back-to-the-land projects have been started by folks dissaffected with urban life. Vegetarians, anarchists, dopeheads, artists, homosexuals, religious groups, and alienated members of the middle class have all tried forms of subsistence agriculture. There are colonies, communes, and individuals out there tending goats from California to Pennsylvania. They bought subscriptions to *Mother Earth News* and *Organic Gardening*, built wigwams, log cabins, geodesic domes, and beer-can houses, and turned out several billion square feet of macrame every year. They grew high-grade dope, put up vegetables by the ton, made candles, and generally once a day discovered something about living on the land that people already knew a hundred years ago. There were democracies, theocracies, patriarchies, matriarchies, childarchies, dopearchies, and a few downright, dagnabbed commie-pinkoarchies. Somehow they got hold of a piece of land somewhere, and would-be pioneers and pioneer-hangers-on tore into it like beavers, injecting it with earthworms and compost, erecting bizarre structures, while they used up whatever capital they brought with them or could beg from relatives in an attempt to "live off the land." You could send twenty kids to Harvard for what it costs to have one try to live off the land for a year. There's all those implements of destruction to buy, water has to come from somewhere, wigwams don't grow on trees, and tires wear out on the minibus going to town for forgotten necessities. It gets to be an expensive scene, man.

If the gardens got planted, and there were no serious social disturbances, these capital inputs could return a substantial chunk of a person's food for a year. It may have cost five dollars a beet to produce, but look at all the fun they had. There was the joy of home canning and the attendant risk of being totaled out by botulism, the thrill of building your own food dryer, the fun of finding ten new recipes for granola, the ecstasy of waiting for the praying mantis eggs to hatch while the chinch bugs ate up the garden. Eventually, usually belatedly, they discovered that the cookie jar had run empty and that the big crash in the macrame market had eliminated the off-farm income supply. There might have been work in town, but if they worked for wages they might as well be living where there are clothes dryers and dishwashers. It got to be a drag eating granola three times a day, and it would have been nice to sneak off and eat a disgustingly unhealthy Big Mac if there were only the money to do it. With communal arrangements some folks get greedy, use too much, or don't do enough. Individuals too often found they had failed to build any more than superficial social relationships with the natives, and that ignorance of local custom can be costly indeed. It is not only a matter of discovering when the first frost might hit. Farmer Smith might need his barn painted and be willing to hire someone to do it. Farmer Brown might also need his barn painted and would hire someone to do it if he could get him to take one of his patented rubber checks. No casual drive through the neighborhood is going to give a clue to who the sharp operators are. Inherited wealth can make anybody look like a financial genius. If the pioneer, in desperation, picks one of these as an adviser on how to make a living in this goddamned place, he won't find out, because his mentor won't have the foggiest idea. He never had to make a living. All he had to do was perform certain functions every year and the money sort of appeared. The real hustler might not appeal to the pilgrim because the hustler is quite likely not only interested in money but fanatical on the subject, appearing crass and commercial. Faced with a dunderhead on the one hand and a barracuda on the other, it is only natural that the poor pilgrim returns to soak up the compounded ignorance of his friends or the intentionally noncommercial contents of his subscriptions. He searches in vain. This type of endeavor is doomed from the start because it is based on the faulty foundation of self-sufficiency as a goal. If we were all Trappist monks, or Amish, we might be able to create a workable model for self-sufficiency.

There are too many ingrained expensive habits for the average person to make a success of subsistence agriculture. Washing clothes on a washboard and hauling water become drudgery eventually, especially when the same tasks can be made comparatively easy by the application of available technology. The doctor may never be called, but there's always the chance someone might get seriously ill, and that takes money. Vehicles of any type need repairs, fuel, tires, and insurance. Staple items, salt, sugar, spices, and so forth, may be cheap compared to prepared foods, but it still takes cash money to buy them. There are always food stamps, of course, but living off the taxpayer doesn't fulfill the goal of self-sufficiency or endear one to the natives. For people who grew up with electricity, the telephone, and indoor plumbing, the crudities of total rusticism quickly wear thin. Every step taken toward civilization takes cash money. Monthly electric bills alone can eat up savings with frightening speed. Wood stoves can be constructed from cheap material, but they are voracious consumers of fuel, and it does not take long to graduate from an ax to a chain saw. Chain saws eat fuel and new chains. Potters and painters need clay, kilns, wheels, paint, and canvas. Even goats have to eat, and if hay is purchased rather than homegrown, the milk will turn out to be rather expensive. In spite of everyone's best intentions, money will eventually become a greater worry than it is for the most jaded urbanite. If no steady supply of funds has been assured, each day will bring an unplanned expense that will create an economic crisis. Pioneering can be a creative, fulfilling endeavor, but being chronically flat broke eliminates the romance in a hurry. Many former commune members are now working on their masters degrees in business administration hoping to land a high-paying corporate job in the city.

More conventional infant small-farm enterprises also tend to suffer from the cash-short syndrome. Too often rookies try to imitate their more established neighbors in the purchase of expensive machinery and the production of capital-intensive cash crops. They rob Peter to pay Paul, and nobody pays Peter. Family living expenses eat up irreplaceable capital, and the farm operation, short of input, loses productivity. If credit is available, it will be used, but not repaid. Eventually the auctioneer will come—to end the struggle. The catechism, "There's no way a young guy can start farming nowadays," will gain added credence as another family slinks off to the city with its tail between its legs.

The real tragedy of this phenomenon is that it is avoidable. Careful preentry planning and preparation can largely eliminate the cash-short syndrome. Patient buildup of resources before attempting full-time farming will provide a firm foundation on which to build further capital acquisition. If the base is sound, real profits will follow. Too often commercial farming or subsistence agriculture is entered into for noneconomic reasons: the romance of growing food, of creating a fresh lifestyle, freedom from urban squalor and vice, release from the pressure of a nine-to-five workday and a cranky boss who fires people for irrational reasons, the need for an open place for children to play safe from child molesters and city traffic. These are all good reasons for moving to the farm, but if they are the basic raison d'etre for the enterprise, it will ultimately fail. The byword should be profit. If adequate income is assured, the rest of the goodies will follow. Relegate profit to secondary consideration, and the joys of rural living will be short-lived indeed.

In recent years the average immigrant to rural life has been a refugee from a high-pressure job in an urban area. He is usually middle-aged and possesses a wide range of skills and a fair amount of capital. He may have spent years planning his move and will be deliberate in constructing his new life. Because of extensive cash resources, he weathers mistakes that would destroy a more impulsive venture. He may have gleaned some unconventional ideas from his reading material over the years and be chomping at the bit to grow organic toadstools, but if the market is not ready he can survive to try something else. This type of pilgrim is likely to socialize with his neighbors because he doesn't necessarily view himself as an oddball. Often these people are highly ambitious and possess such highly visible management skills that they end up serving their adopted neighborhoods as elected officials. These individuals have the rare ability to blend a fresh viewpoint with existing local realities and create an agricultural venture which can be both revolutionary and profitable.

Self-Evaluation

If the urge to own a gerbil ranch occupies your waking thoughts, or if you find yourself weeding strawberries in your sleep, if you find yourself at work daydreaming about sweet-smelling wood fires and verdant tree-lined valleys, you have been hit by the back-to-the-boondocks syndrome, and, unfortunately, there is no known cure aside from actual experience. Before the attacks become so powerful that you abandon all reason and go shopping for a chain saw, it is crucial that you take a personal inventory. Do you finish projects once begun, or does adversity stifle your enthusiasm? Can you comprehend what you read, or do you rely on concrete example or oral instruction to learn new skills? How dependent are you on authority figures? Could you really run your boss's business as well as he, or do you find yourself relieved when someone else takes ultimate responsibility for your mistakes? Do you handle difficult situations by retreating or acting passive until they go away, or do you manipulate actively in an attempt to reach a satisfactory conclusion? How easily do you make new friends? If you are a social retard, is it by choice or natural development? If other people would be involved in the endeavor, friends, husbands, wives, children, how do they stack up? Do they share your enthusiasms, or do they humor you as a lovable eccentric? What are your marketable skills? What sort of work are you willing to do? If you are an accountant, would you be willing to be a bookkeeper in a country elevator at a cut in pay? If you are in management, could you change tires to earn extra money? Can you give dancing lessons, pound nails, or fix leaky plumbing? How you answer these questions will give a good indication of your suitability as farmer material.

Finally, since capital accumulation is the ultimate financial goal of the farming game, how good is your basic knowledge of the principles of capitalism? Does "buying cheap and selling dear" ring a bell? Does "cost of production" sound familiar? The finest example of farmer-capitalism I have known, B. J. Tupper, has said more than once, "I wouldn't know enough to run a popcorn wagon, but I've never seen anybody get rich working for wages." Upon hearing that, do you find hundreds of examples of rich wage earners passing between your ears, or do you nod and say, "Ah-ha, I believe that fellow has something there"? Rich to a wage-freak means having lots of money to spend on himself. Rich to a capitalist means adequate funds to invest in schemes to produce profits that can be invested in other schemes. Personal expenses are more of a bother than a pleasure, and each one is mentally subtracted from the available investment-capital supply. For the noncapitalist, a trip to Europe means spending surplus money for travel rather than something else, like a different car. For the capitalist, the same trip would cost future investment opportunity and a loss of potential profit down the road. It is not a decision to be made lightly just because the money happens to be in the checking account this week. People who invest in the stock market are usually not capitalists but investors. To put money to work in the hope it will pay dividends and increase in value is a far different proposition from involving oneself in the day-to-day manipulation of the investment. If you are not conversant with the principles of such endeavor, it would be well to give them some serious study.

Getting Started

Nithe little plathe you got here. Putty far up in the woodth though. Latht feller to live here went crazy and they put him away.

Paw Kettle, *The Egg and I*,
Betty McDonald

I am going to assume the potential farmer has some money

to invest, either in liquid assets (stocks, bonds, savings accounts) or some property equity that can be recovered through sale (a house, condominium, second car). The amount of these funds will determine, to some extent, what sort of farm you can afford. In some parts of the country 20- and 40-acre parcels are still available. On the Great Plains they are rare and can usually be purchased only if a landowner will split a larger piece of land. This need not be a problem if total cost is considered. In northern Indiana a 20-acre farm with a good set of buildings might fetch $100,000. In central Kansas a 160-acre farm with buildings could be purchased for $56,000. In the same area of Kansas a 20-acre parcel might bring $40,000, so it may be cheaper to buy the larger acreage. Generally, the smaller the parcel, the higher the price per acre. If 80 acres can be bought on contract for $400 an acre, the total cost would be $32,000. A down payment of 20 percent would require $9,280, and yearly payments and interest at 12 percent over twenty years would average around $3,000 per year. (That's $250 a month for those in the habit.) One of the better buys in the past year was purchased in northcentral Kansas. It was 40 acres with a solid house and good out-buildings for $16,000— $3,200 down and the balance over twenty years at 10 percent, or $160 a month.

The closer a farm is to a city, the higher the price. This is where some serious investigation comes into play. If you will require $12,000 a year in off-farm income for five years to get established and your job of choice is fifty miles of bad road from the selected farm, either the job or the farm should be reexamined. An acreage a few miles off the main road will have a cheaper price tag than one on the highway, and four-wheel-drive pickups can go amazing places. After living in an area for a few months, you may find attractive job opportunities opening up in the neighborhood, eliminating extended commuting. A low-risk method of getting a farm would be to select an area and rent a house and set of buildings for a while. On the High Plains these can be had for $60 a month. Rental would give the would-be pilgrim the chance to try his hand at live-stock and he could build a herd of sows, for instance, without the burden of land payments. While renting, there would be time and opportunity to thoroughly scout the area for good buys, which sometimes come up only every two years or so. It may be found for some reason that the initial geographic choice is unsuitable or that the farming game is not what it's cracked up to be, in which case not much has been lost.

Good neighbors are essential to long-term contentment with a farm. Feuds can last for years and cast a permanent pall on life in general. It is easier to buy after getting an accurate reading on the neighborhood than it is to pull out of a nasty social situation once the farm is purchased. You may be able to laugh off the creep that lives down the road for a while, but eventually he'll get on your nerves.

Good value in a farm means different things to different people. Some salivate over a well-kept house with petunia beds. Others love flat fields of deep rich soil. My own preju-dices favor a farm with a good number of structurally sound outbuildings (they do not have to be painted), a source of ade-quate water, either spring or underground, and some arable land. An 80-acre farm with only 20 acres of arable land will sell at a more reasonable price than one that is all tillable, and 20 acres can produce enough roughage to keep quite a number of animals alive over the winter. Houses are not a major consid-eration, although the less repair they need the better. Nobody makes any money with a dwelling unless he rents it out. Out-buildings can house profitable enterprises, and a small farmer always finds himself short on shelter for his animals. That small chicken house over there can make $1,000 a year if used for baby calves; the hog house under the big tree could house 10 sows at a time, and that's 400 pigs a year at $25 apiece profit is. . . . Houses for people simply do not compute. Animals come first. In this regard, adequate water cannot be overemphasized. Limited water means fewer animals, and that eventuates in smaller profits. Hard water is not a serious problem. Water loaded with nitrates can cause infertility, abortion, and slow rate of gain. Nitrate content can vary widely within a small area, so this needs to be checked carefully.* Rough land should be viewed primarily as summer grass for ruminants but can be used for warm-weather farrowing for hogs or as the site of a potential orchard. Rough land with ponds for livestock water is preferred. Pasture with running water is ideal. Subirrigated creek bottoms supply grass even during severe drought, and running water may be diverted to supply cheap irrigation for crops. Good fences are worth forty dollars an acre over poor ones, with the cost of posts and wire going up every year.

Having rented a suitable farmstead or taken the major step of purchasing, the pilgrim may need to secure a source of off-farm income if he has not already done so. Self-employment opportunities include odd jobs, carpentry, plumbing, electrical work, feed sales, and lesson giving (piano, guitar, voice, art, and so forth). For around $5,000 a small skid loader can be purchased that can clean out barns and corrals at the rate of $20 an hour. These machines are very dependable and require few repairs. Most farmers would hire this work done if given the opportunity, but if there are several loaders for hire in the neighborhood, the market may be saturated. Small trenching machines are profitable, low-investment ventures and are usually used in an automatic-waterer installation business. A person with any understanding of plumbing can make good wages selling and installing these increasingly popular devices. The machinery can be bought for the price of one water system and can be used any time weather permits to earn extra in-

---

* Some nitrate effects can be counteracted by feeding liberal supplements of Vitamin A.

come. Salaried jobs are usually not hard to find in rural areas, but the wages tend to be lower than city rates. The exceptions are government work and teaching positions. Truck-driving jobs are plentiful and there is usually seasonal harvest work to be had.

Good hired men draw $800 to $1,200 a month, usually with house and utilities furnished. Totally unskilled farm workers could probably find a patient farmer who would require simple tasks to start, like discing summer fallow, in return for a fairly low hourly wage. This form of employment, if the pilgrim can afford it, would provide the necessary experience most rookies lack. There is nothing particularly demanding about field work, once tractor and operator are familiar with each other. During the learning period, however, there is always a chance that a rookie will allow a $30,000 tractor to run low on oil, ruining the engine, or will slam a $6,000 disc into a telephone pole. The following example should suffice in demonstrating the risks farmers assume in hiring rookie labor.

An acquaintance once hired a high school kid for the summer. Everything went smoothly at first, since the kid was afraid of making a mistake and approached each job cautiously. Gradually he gained confidence, and boyish enthusiasm overcame his unnatural conservatism. In the space of one week, he mired a four-wheel-drive pickup at the wet end of an irrigated cornfield, broke three $80 shanks from a chisel plow, wrapped a half mile of woven wire fence in a field cultivator and pulled it halfway across the section without noticing, and drove the teeth of a Farmhand loader into a hard-pan gravel road while traveling in road gear. In desperation, the farmer put the kid on a tractor with a disc and told him to run over the summer fallow and not to break anything. Working summer fallow is usually a simple task with few demands other than keeping awake. The kid, determined to redeem himself, concentrated mightily on the work. He slowed on each turn, making sure the end gangs cleared the fences. He listened to the engine for any signs of distress. In fact, he was so intent on his job that he became fascinated with the smoke pouring from the exhaust at the front of the tractor; in time he became transfixed. A large electric pole passing a few inches from his right rear tire caught his attention briefly, but as the tractor squeezed past, he breathed a sigh of relief, forgetting the disc behind was twice the width of the tractor. The collision spun him halfway around the pole, clipping the two outside gangs from the disc and bending the hitch into a U. Using wire and some extra bolts from the tool box, the kid managed to get the disc back together enough to pull it home. As it happened to be lunch time, he parked out of sight from the house and sneaked in to eat. After washing down dessert with the last glass of iced tea, he informed his boss that he'd had a little trouble on the road and that a wild driver had forced him into the ditch, doing minor damage to the disc. Thinking the kid had overestimated the damage because of his recent accidents, the farmer walked out to look at the situation. When he returned he sat at the table with his head in his hands for twenty minutes without saying a word. Finally, tension got to the kid and he began railing at the crazy drivers in the neighborhood who had no consideration for hard-working farmers.

The farmer lifted a hand and began in a controlled voice, "Bill, I guess you're about the best hired man I've ever had. You put in a good day's work. You never complain about a job no matter how dirty. If I didn't pull you off the tractor in the evening you might work all night. You're a good hand with livestock, and you've always got a joke or a story that makes working with you a lot of fun. But by God, Bill, I think you could screw up a crowbar!"

The kid is now farming his own land, putting in long hours one day and fixing what he tears up the next. He never did learn caution but can make most repairs himself. If the truth were known, he has successfully fixed more complicated break-downs than many an experienced mechanic.

Once a source of off-farm income is secured and a base of operations established, on-farm production of food and energy should begin. Basic living costs can be dramatically reduced by the shrewd application of available technology without lowering the standard of living. On-farm production of food will, in most cases, actually improve the quality and diversity of the average diet.

A reduction in expenditures for energy inputs begins with conservation. Most older farm homes need to be insulated and have windows and doors sealed or replaced. Foundations may need repair or may benefit from insulating procedures. Solar window-box heat collectors can be constructed for minimal cost and, depending on size and placement, can provide major portions of daytime heating requirements. For about two hundred dollars, the south wall of a house may be covered with a solar collector that will heat the entire home. Efficient wood stoves can be built to meet the balance of home heating needs in areas where wood is plentiful. Where wood is in short supply, large furnaces placed outside the home can be constructed that burn large, round bales of straw, dry weeds, or crop residues and require replenishment only once a week or so. If the fuel crop were to be produced on-farm and the baling work custom hired, the cost per month would run to about twenty dollars for the coldest months. By adding solar heating technology, such a system could be made to function at ten dollars per month.

A greenhouse built on a dwelling's south side can provide tomatoes, lettuce, and other table greens the entire winter. Because produce prices trend seasonally higher in the winter, this can represent a substantial savings. Garden plants (tomatoes, peppers, cabbage) can be started here in the late winter for the home garden. Moreover, if properly designed, the greenhouse can supply a good portion of the daytime winter heat for the home, acting as a huge solar collector.

Long-range planning is necessary to maximize home food production, particularly where orchard and berry enterprise is contemplated. Since such an operation may take from five to ten years to reach full production, locating and positioning the various seedlings need to be done with great care. Proximity to supplemental water cannot be overemphasized. The tastes and needs of the living unit must be supplied first. Once this is done by full-range selection of fruit trees and berry bushes, attention should focus on cash-crop potential in some particular plants. Blueberries and strawberries are well suited to expansion for income and work well in tandem. In most areas of the High Plains these items are in short supply, and people will drive miles to pick their own. Both require intense farming practices and irrigation, but income potential is little short of astronomical. Once a pick-it-yourself business is established, other items such as cantaloupe, apples, and plums will begin to sell on the same basis. Strawberries can be ready for full production the year after they are planted and are usually torn up and replanted every second or third year. Three beds can be laid out and rotated so there is a constant supply of berries. Yields under good management range from 4,000 to 5,000 quarts per acre, which at 50 cents per quart would yield a gross income per acre of $2,000 to $2,500. With such profit potential it would be tempting to plant everything to strawberries, but this would be a mistake. It is best to start small, learning the business, and vital not to grow so large that the local market will no longer accommodate the crop. Much better to have some customers unable to get strawberries than to become dependent on hired labor to pick the crop and on unstable distant markets, where transportation can eat up profits. Blueberry bushes need from five to seven years to mature. Meanwhile they require yearly pruning and water. Soil PH needs careful attention and may have to be adjusted from time to time. Once in production, blueberries yield from thirty-five to fifty pounds per plant and bear fruit for one hundred years or more. Set out in a small space, seedlings need to be replanted at a rate of 600 plants per acre. By starting new seedling beds every year, the population can be expanded gradually to meet demand and growing expertise. Ten acres of blueberries will be about as much as one family can handle. Bees are essential to blueberry production, and blueberry honey brings a premium price. Since bees are also yield boosters in other areas of fruit production, their husbandry and the intricacies of honey marketing should be studied at length with an eye to including bees as a profitable sideline. If an acre of blueberries were to yield forty pounds per plant at 40 cents a pound, and there were 600 plants, the per-acre gross income would come to $9,600. Until recently blueberry production was limited to certain areas of the country. However, now varieties have been developed for almost all of the continental United States, and blueberry-pie fanciers all over the country are waiting impatiently for farmers to get with it. Who are we to deny them?

Twenty acres devoted to blueberries, strawberries, apples, and other fruit trees should eventually produce a gross income exceeding $100,000. Expenses will vary, but $50,000 net would be conservative. Furthermore, the value of the farm will rise in reflection of its earning power. Raw land fully converted will appreciate by a factor of ten, effectively doubling net income for the first ten years.

Assuming some orchard production is kept for home use, a small vegetable garden should supply the balance of nonmeat and milk diet items. Solar food drying is the cheapest form of food preservation, but canning and freezing may also be used.

Twenty acres of orchard and garden in full production will keep a couple of people well occupied for four to five months out of the year. If this route is chosen, there are several livestock enterprises that will fit in nicely and provide winter income as well.

Geese do well in orchards and keep the weed and insect populations under control. After grazing out the orchard, the geese should be finished on a grain ration and sold. If a market can be found for the birds, this can develop into a nice sideline.

Sheep can perform the same function as geese, although very young trees need the wire or treated burlap protection used for rabbits. Utilizing land for double production (fruit and sheep) increases gross income and lowers the cost of production for both.

Swine will enjoy any windfall or overripe fruit. Even if the volume of such food is small, it will stimulate appetite for grain, and weight gains will be more rapid. Some farmers in Missouri "hog down" all windfall peaches while farrowing on pasture in the fall. Excess garden greens, over-mature sweet corn, as well as leftover material from canning and freezing operations can fatten several pigs.

A solar-heated farrowing house or adapted barn can house enough sows at a reasonable cost to furnish a steady cash flow through the winter months. Started on a small basis with two or three sows, the operation can be expanded to fit expertise and available space. By the time two or three litters are farrowed, a rookie should have an idea whether he is cut out for the business. If results are unsatisfactory, or hog raising is depressing, get out before too much capital is invested. This rule applies to all farm ventures. Get in small, work out the problems, and do those things that are satisfying and profitable. Never attempt to jump in on a scale that would threaten the whole venture if it went sour.

Milk cows have a place on most small farms. A minimum of two is required to assure a year-round supply of dairy products. Milk, cream, butter, cheese, yogurt, custard, and ice cream produced on the farm can cut a large chunk out of the grocery bill. Excess milk and cream can be sold or traded for eggs. Purchase of a separator (a good one brings $25 at a farm sale) allows skim milk to be fed to calves or small pigs. If roughage is grown on the farm and grain and concentrate purchased, the price of milk produced will compare with store costs. However, all other dairy products obtained will be free. Skim milk can turn weak, weird-looking pigs into market toppers. Bull calves from the milk cows, castrated and fattened, add to the family's food supply. Heifer calves raised and bred can be added to the herd or sold at a premium. Gentle family milk cows are in good demand.

Personally, I am prejudiced toward the Jersey breed because of high butterfat content relative to volume and low daily maintenance requirements. Guernseys are larger animals and fully as gentle but also eat more. Ayrshire, Brown Swiss, and Holsteins are more suited to full-scale dairy operations where whole milk is sold and large quantities of cheap roughage are available. These animals are more apt to be contrary, and their milk in no way compares in quality with Jersey or Guernsey production. Jerseys mature early, have few calving problems, and generally breed back quickly. They also can be intimidated by larger breeds, so it is not a good idea to mix them with, say, Holsteins. Like all milk cows, Jerseys need to be handled gently. Cows can hold grudges for a remarkably long time, so it is best to be patient. Lose your temper, and a milk cow will repay you several times for the error. She will dirty the milking parlor, nail you with a wet tail, or absentmindedly step in a bucket of milk. Time means nothing to an irritated cow. She may wait a couple of weeks to take her revenge. If you can control your temper, approaching each milking with an attitude of sweetness and light, your cows will give more milk and show you the greatest consideration and, in time, affection. Milking cows will keep you home and deter foolish expenditure of money. They also supply the secret ingredient for success in the pig-scalping business (skim milk, whey, and butter-milk). By following Sherman's methods to the letter, you can make this little sideline perform admirably, especially if you devote a few years to practice.

If milk cows, sheep, or other ruminants are to be an integral part of an operation, a plentiful supply of roughage should be grown on the farm. Alfalfa is the crop of choice since it provides almost a complete diet for most ruminants and improves the soil in which it is grown. Twenty acres of irrigated alfalfa will produce at least one hundred tons in most years. In years of adequate rainfall, dryland alfalfa will produce from three to four tons per acre on the High Plains. Sudan grass performs better than alfalfa in hot, dry conditions. A crop rotation including both of these crops every year will help assure a supply of feed even during drouth years, as will the continuous practice of adding humus to the soil (green manure, compost, and so forth), thereby increasing water-holding capabilities as well as fertility.

In summary, a basic production unit should contain an orchard, a garden space, a greenhouse, and sufficient land devoted to the production of roughage to supply the anticipated needs of the ruminant population. An ideal crop rotation would include alfalfa, sweet clover (for plow-down green manure), sudan grass, and oats. A few sows, a couple of milk cows, and a small flock of sheep will allow full utilization of waste resources (scraps, windfall fruit, rough grazing land, and milk by-products) and keep the table supplied with meat. Excess production can be sold to help meet expenses.

Every effort should be made to make the unit energy self-sufficient. Since the cheapest, simplest technology available applies to solar heat production, this means insulating buildings and constructing the various forms of collectors that prove suited to the particular operation.

With such a base in place, the basic cash outflow of the unit will be reduced to manageable proportions. Land payments, transportation, electricity, clothing, health insurance, and entertainment costs will represent the major remaining cash expenditures. At today's prices these costs will range from $12,000 to $18,000, depending on the size of the living unit and the general thriftiness of the operator. A good source of off-farm income should meet these expenses while the rookie is developing his operation into a full-time project.

We have already discussed hog farrowing, pig scalping, and orchard, bee, and berry production. There are several other enterprises which are suited to the small-farm operation.

Greenhouse

By starting with the family greenhouse, you may discover a nearby market hungry for your excess production. Leaf lettuce is generally in good demand during the winter months. Flowers, bedding plants, and tomatoes should not be overlooked. Spring garden plants (cabbages, peppers, tomatoes, onions) find a ready outlet in most areas. They can be sold for a few cents under the Earl-May price and still deliver attractive profits. If the market looks promising for these ventures, it may pay to expand greenhouse capacity. Full-size, free-standing commercial greenhouses take big bucks to construct and are expensive to heat. These costs can be dramatically reduced by using the south walls of existing buildings, digging the floor level down five feet into the ground, and including solar-heating technology. Lower production expenses allow profits to accrue at small sales volumes. Going the lean-to greenhouse route lowers entrance-capital requirements and permits orderly expansion. The possibility remains that a successfully operated business may require a huge conventional energy-gobbling monstrosity at some future point. If this seems to be the case, remember Paw Kettle's admonition, "Jutht remember, thon, you pay for your own funral." Any time the greenhouse business undergoes economic stress, you will suffer according to the amount of money you have bet. Perhaps the Gammaglobulin corpus delecti eatus muchas beetle will infest your new acre-under-one-roof plant heaven. Clearing the little devils out may well mean junking all existing plants, spraying unmentionable substances about, and starting over from scratch. This would result in a total loss of cash sales for at least a month. If the operation remains diversified in several, small lean-to structures, banzai attacks by the dreaded Bolshoi borscht invectum worm or the pesky Leaf blightus blottus rustoleumus can be localized and dealt with in the severe manner they deserve without crunching the cash flow.

Development of a nursery featuring trees and ornamental shrubs can dovetail with the greenhouse business. Folks in the habit of stopping by for the latest in cabbage slawvinus will be good prospects for quaking willows and weeping aspens. Throw in berry picking in the summer and apple harvest in the fall, and you'll have more customers than Irma La Douce.

Pets

In some rural areas of the country the loss of income from the sale of cream and eggs has been replaced by the production of animals and birds for the wholesale pet trade. Because recently the government has put some embargoes on the importation of birds, new opportunities have opened up for domestic bird raisers. Singing canaries can fetch upwards of $80 wholesale and parrots well over $100. Getting these birds to breed in captivity is no small trick and usually involves setting up a large greenhouse affair closely approximating natural conditions. Adequate distance between floor and roof is essential.

Considering that the environments for successful bird husbandry and the production of some houseplants are identical, the two operations may be combined to spread overhead costs.

Dogs

Dogs may have a limited future market as more cities emulate New York's stiff scoop-the-poop laws. However, with rising feed costs and increasing federal red tape, demand for certain breeds will tend to outrun supply. Toy breeds and terrier types sell at a ratio of roughly four to one to large breeds like German shepherds and Saint Bernards. A well-managed, disease-free kennel can expect to net 100 percent of investment each year, especially if superior bloodlines are purchased for breeding stock. The dog business has attracted more than its share of fast-buck artists. Horror stories of unsanitary "puppy mills" abound. Buy sound, representative stock from a reputable commercial kennel, provide a clean, healthy environment with some care and affection, and you will be producing quality merchandise with a good outlet. Eighty-five percent of the dogs sold as pets in this country come from commercial kennels. Some of these outfits are pig sties where no attention is paid to who fathered whom or what disease killed what. This type of operation cannot survive the high cost of dog food or the inspections of USDA officials. Most commercial kennels of any volume are highly sophisticated and require the same managerial skills necessary for the success of any livestock enterprise. A basic knowledge of canine disease, nutrition, and reproductive processes is essential. Marketing skills are vital. The best way to learn the business is to go to a successful operator and pump his brain pan dry. Unfortunately, most of the outstanding commercial kennels are located in a small area of northcentral Kansas. If your heart is set on going to the dogs, it would be worth your while to look up one of these folks.

Trailane Kennels at Soldier, Kansas, and C and R Kennels at Barnes, Kansas, are the best in the business, but there are several others in the area almost as good. A survey of pet stores can give a good idea of which breeds are moving well.

Do not under any circumstances confuse the commercial dog business with the show-dog business. The chasm between the two is insurmountable. Show-dog people look upon the commercial kennel as an unpleasant form of lice and have been striving mightily for several years to eliminate the competition. A few trips around the show ring with a pedigreed canine, and these folks undergo a remarkable transformation. Their noses begin to point skyward, they hone their backstabbing skills to the utmost, and they practice chicanery and skullduggery of the basest sort. Lucretia Borgia on attending a purebred dog show, would, no doubt, feel compelled to join a Brownie Scout troop for protection. Dogs with hip dysplasia come home with trophies galore. A bloodline may be particularly vicious, but have the ace handler show the dog and have the right judge in the ring, and the points will accrue. No commercial kennel of reputation would ever breed a dysplastic dog. Show folks, who claim to be in the dog business "to improve the breed" would not hesitate at breeding a Saint Bernard to a mountain lion if the fee were right. I have had the misfortune of seeing the worst of both worlds. There was a commercial kennel in Iowa where nine out of ten puppies died of hookworms before they were four weeks old. Bitches were whelped in a pile of newspapers in the basement of the house. The pile grew with the years. Fleas, ear mites, ticks, and mange of every description flourished. The dogs were undernourished but at least had adequate exercise area and shelter. This kennel no longer exists.

The worst show kennel I ever hope to see was located in southeastern Wisconsin. The woman in charge had put together an outstanding collection of bloodlines for her chosen breed of dog. Many of these bloodlines were unavailable to commercial kennels because of snobbery. Her dogs, all sixty-five of them, lived in a fenced-in yard of about two and half acres. Most were missing an ear, some two, as sixty-five dogs will have their social problems now and then. No one knew which of the twenty-odd males had bred which of the forty-odd females when or how many times. It's quite difficult to keep bloodlines straight in such circumstances. The whelping area turned out to be the woman's home (defined loosely). Dog excrement was piled two feet high from the kitchen to the front door. The ammonia supply, if harnessed, would have freed us from dependence on Arab oil. The only furniture un-scathed was the trophy case, which was loaded. Last I heard she was still on the circuit with her one-eared wonders.

The well-run commercial kennel remains the project of choice for the fledgling dog breeder. Much less chance of poisoned soup, and the pay is better. Do your homework and build a reputation for honesty and quality, and profits will follow.

Dogs go in and out of style overnight. If Jackie Kennedy buys a Maltese, half the Eastern Seaboard will crave the little brutes. Have Diane von Furstenburg exercise a Mexican hairless, and no kennel south of the Rio Grande will be safe from marauding socialites. Guessing on fashion trends can be a dangerous game, as those folks who plunked down $500 a crack for Shih Tzu breeding stock will tell you. There are several breeds that have retained their popularity and price for a number of years. These are the best bets, although each has its peculiar problems.

Terriers

West Highland White	Cairn
Scottish	Silky
Yorkshire	Miniature Schnauzer

Other

Lhasa Apso	Samoyed
Pekinese	Keeshound
Pomeranian	Shetland Sheepdog
Cocker Spaniel	Pug
English Bulldog	

The best procedure upon selecting a breed is to purchase the best male puppy you can find. Since males generally mature more slowly than females, he will need a head start on any females purchased. One male and three females would be a good beginning. In two years' time you should have enough puppies to begin building a reputation. If the project works out, you can add other breeds to your line. Generally speaking, offering more breeds will increase customer interest. There are very few pet stores that can absorb entire litters of a given breed. Commonly they want a pair of each of several breeds. By ordering several puppies from one place they save on telephone and shipping expenses.

Shipping problems have threatened the existence of the dog business for the past several years. Vague USDA rules have made pet freight unpopular with airlines, and crating requirements change frequently. The best procedure for alleviating problems is to go to the airport you will be using and befriend the personnel. Anything you can do to make their job easier will most times be rewarded with better service. Little tips from them can help you avoid costly mistakes (chiefly returned puppies for improper crating and temperature violations). All puppies should be shipped C.O.D. Most pet store operators are as honest as the next fellow, but the attrition rate in the retail pet business is awesome. Bankrupt firms are hesitant to pay for merchandise if it can be avoided.

Some dog raisers sell puppies to brokers, thereby avoiding

the hassles of air shipment and the overhead costs of many long-distance phone calls. A relationship with a reputable dog broker is perhaps the best way to break into merchandising. The price offered will not be too attractive, but puppies can be sold in litter lots at weaning age at the cost of one phone call. Dog brokers make money on the difference between litter-lot price and the wholesale price to pet stores. They need about $15 a puppy to break even. On some breeds the markup will run to $50 or more. Large brokers may handle over five thousand puppies a year. The waters are full of sharks, however. Some of the greasiest characters imaginable have been attracted to the dog business from time to time. They promise to pay at a future date, or they dock the price from that stated on the phone. One infamous broker in Nebraska once burned a whole warehouse full of puppies to collect on the insurance. Upon meeting up with these vermin, shoot on sight. Under no circumstances do any business with them. Area dog breeders will know a trustworthy broker, so, hopefully, you can avoid contact with the slimeball element.

Eventually you will want to sell puppies directly to pet stores, for the money is much better. As you broaden your markets it is still important to keep your broker happy. Someday you may have fifty Lhasa Apsos eating you out of house and home and will need him.

Cats

Registered cats are an attractive investment. They carry high price tags, and the potential market is broader than the dog market. Many more folks have room for a cat than have space for a dog. Burmese and Persians have moved well lately, although Manx and Siamese have been steady over the years.

Cat food is more expensive than dog food, but, of course, it takes relatively small amounts to keep our feline friends in the pink. Cats and dogs do not mix well, outside of several Albanian porridges, but if kept in separate facilities, they can augment each other in the pet trade. The same pet shop that takes six dogs may want twelve cats. It saves phone calls.

Guinea Pigs

Guinea pigs need to be raised in addition to other pets. Their price is too low to justify much of a telephone bill in merchandising them. I once met a man with 4,000 guinea pig sows, but he also had 450 dogs to help him sell his guinea pigs. With the demise of the pet turtle (salmonella problems) as the overwhelming choice as Junior's first pet, the guinea pig has moved into the spotlight. Your average, run-of-mill pig will fetch $5 wholesale. Exotics like Peruvians and Rosettes can bring $15 at the right store. Slip a dozen of the little devils into each dog shipment, and $5 each will begin to amount to something.

Small wooden boxes filled with clover and grass hay make the best homes for cavies. Colonies of one boar and three sows seem to work best, as all adults care for all piglets, regardless of parentage. Guinea pigs don't eat much, grain and alfalfa pellets being popular choices, and are prone to reproduce at remarkable levels. Ten litters per year per sow would not be unusual. The life expectancy of Guinea pigs is rather limited. This means pets are constantly being replaced, which makes for a healthy market, but also means that breeding stock is a short-term investment. If you can grow carrots on your farm, they can be added to the pigs' diet to improve longevity. A carrot a day will up your piggy production and should add a year to the life expectancy of each brood sow. Since each sow should return $150 in net income each year, the cavies earn their keep.

Ferrets

Domesticated ferrets are becoming popular pets in many areas of the country. They are also handy for rat eradication, because they can pop down a rathole and clean up the whole mess in a few minutes. Ferrets are affectionate and clean by nature, in addition to their ferocious antirat propensities. Ferrets have six to twelve offspring every year. They are handled much like cats but need a high level of meat in their diets. Baby ferrets bring from $20 to $35 each. With feed and housing costs somewhat variable, each female ferret should return about $200 per year in net income. One hundred ferret females make a tidy unit and can be housed in one small building. However, do not put guinea pigs and ferrets in the same facility or there will be hell to pay.

As rats continue to develop immunity to poisons, ferrets will experience increasing demand as rodent assassins. When their value is fully appreciated by the market, the price should move up accordingly. At this writing the future of the ferret business looks rosy indeed.

A profitable sideline for the ferret baron could be custom rat removal. Since ferrets can be trained to come back to the owner, they can be taken to strange surroundings, unleashed on the unsuspecting rats, and be called back when the mayhem is completed. If you have priced the services of a professional exterminator lately, it should be clear how a couple of well-trained ferrets could perk up the old cash flow.

All phases of the pet business require better-than-average management ability and put a premium on marketing skills. Sound breeding stock is essential, and considerable research should be done before any purchases are made. Energy-efficient housing can make or break a rookie venture, so proper planning in that direction should be emphasized. Produce a quality product, market at a fair price, keep fixed costs low, and the profit margins will be astounding.

Sheep

The best way to biggest profits in the sheep business for an operator with limited carrying capacity is to buy superior registered breeding stock and cater to the 4-H club lamb market. A small farm of forty acres may have only enough roughage and pasture for twenty ewes. Potential income can be doubled or even tripled by producing potential prize-winning feeder lambs. With proper advertising and marketing, twenty ewes can produce close to $2,000 in net income. It may be necessary to win some prizes of your own to command this kind of price, but the money spent on exhibition will be a wise investment in the long run.

Goats

Registered dairy goats have undergone a surge in popularity in recent years. Prices of up to $400 have been paid for a particularly productive bloodline. The main problem with high-priced goats is that there are limited numbers of people willing to pay up for them. Sold at a livestock auction, a $400-goat may bring $1.50. With marketing a major problem, goats remain a very tenuous venture for most people. There are some exceptions. If a market can be found for goat milk, the productive capabilities of the dairy nanny will quickly produce profits. Sherman the Scalper milks goats to assist his calf-scalping business. Mohair goats can be fed subsistence rations and sheared twice a year. An abundance of rough, forested land on a farm could be devoted to mohair production. Labor costs are low, and the price of mohair is climbing.

Fish

Fish farming has received limited attention from farmers and the USDA. Most development of the industry has taken place in the Deep South where the length of the growing season allows fish to grow rapidly. There is no reason, however, why farm ponds in all areas of the country cannot be adapted to fish production. Catfish raising is the most popular choice, but trout, bass, perch, and bait minnows also have their advocates. Best results are obtained with a constant supply of fresh water provided by springs, wells, or stream diversion. Where supplemental water is impossible to establish, stocking rates can be lowered to conform with carrying capacity. The important thing to remember is that any permanent body of water, no matter how small, can be made to produce income. Fingerlings can be started in small ponds and transferred later to larger ones or sold as stocking fish to other growers.

The best setups use a series of descending ponds in which the overflow from one pond goes into the next, and so on. One source can supply all of the ponds with cool, oxygen-laden water. Timed self-feeders can be set up for each pond or the fish can be fed by hand. To ease harvesting and cleaning, ponds built specifically for the purpose have drains which are opened to lower the water levels. Generally speaking, the greater the number of ponds, the more opportunities available for diversification. Reliance on one species of fish is likely to result in economic adversity if weather or market conditions are hostile. A balanced operation will include fish for bait, table, and stocking.

The two most serious problems of fish farming are energy

costs for water pumping and marketing. Spring water or a diverted stream can help solve the first problem. Small ponds may be fed by windmill-pumped water. The second problem takes ingenuity and hard work.

Some areas have facilities that buy live fish from the farmer and do all cleaning, packaging, and marketing. As aquaculture becomes common, more farmer-owned cooperative packing and marketing plants will be built. In the meantime, most fish farmers must rely on self-developed markets to absorb their production. Portable truck-mounted water tanks are necessary for volume sales. Minnow and crawfish are usually sold on a "route" of baitshops located near sportfishing areas. Weekly deliveries are required during the summer months. Trout can be sold live by setting up fishing ponds at conventions and expositions and charging for each fish caught. Likewise, stocking fish need to be transported in good condition if repeat business is to be assured.

The sale of dressed fish to restaurants is a highly profitable enterprise but requires the construction of facilities for dressing and quick-freezing. The monotony of cleaning fish may put a strain on family relationships. Fish eyes have a way of depressing viewers, making them irritable and balky. Inevitably, if production grows, labor must be hired, and this means dealing with all the problems and expense inherent in becoming an employer. The problems may be duck soup to some but are insurmountable to most, which is why most of the world now works for wages. Cooperative fish-processing ventures will be needed before fish farming becomes fully exploited as a source of income.

One of the more exciting possibilities in fish marketing is the production of the breaded squares of fabricated fish that go into the "fish sandwich" sold around the country. Machinery for the enterprise is not cheap, but the potential payoff is enormous. Almost any sort of fish can be used, including the much-maligned carp. Sold as fish cakes to restaurants, grocery stores, and individuals, carp would carry a higher price tag per pound than rainbow trout. Perch and carp, both well adapted to warmer water temperatures than bass or trout, can be raised under less than perfect conditions at a lower cost per pound than most other fish. Once they are fabricated, breaded, cooked, and placed on a sesame seed bun with tartar sauce, no one can tell but what they are really cod fish or walleye. With rising transportation costs and wholesale seafood costs pushing the price of these precocious patties into the stratosphere, a locally grown-and-packaged product will find it can undersell the competition with enough profit left to help with the inevitable attacks of fisheye phobia.

Cattle

I have mentioned the pervasive condition of unbalanced mind afflicting cattlemen. They are crazy, pure and simple. If you are not already discouraged from attempting this enterprise, do not blame me. I did my best.

Sheep and cattle consume the same forms of sustenance. Cattle are inefficient in comparison because of the multiple births of sheep and their lower maintenance requirements. However, sheep do have their faults. They consider stupidity a virtue. Dropping dead for no apparent reason is their national sport. Coyotes and neighborhood dogs get a kick out of killing great numbers of sheep in a short period of time. A coyote loose in a flock of sheep can wipe out a whole year's profits in a few minutes. Sheep also require more labor than cattle. For these reasons there may be some rational reasons for turning to cattle as a small-farm enterprise. To my mind, the reasoning is weak when the greater profit potential of sheep is added to the equation, but if you are afflicted with cattle-mania, the case is hopeless.

Cattlemen have been trying to turn a profit ever since the

glory days of the Texas trail drive, usually without success. If your farm has some pasture land that cannot be converted to other uses, if you have access to cornstalks or other cheap winter grazing, and if there is sufficient farmland to grow hay crops, a bare possibility of profit exists. An average herd of cattle with average calf production is still going to lose money, but the bite will not be so serious. As with a small flock of sheep, the emphasis should be on quality. In the Sandhills of Nebraska there is a cattleman with fifteen cows who consistently tops nationally known purebred sales every year. He has accomplished this amazing feat by culling any cows that do not wean a 600-pound calf at 205 days of age (an average calf might weigh 420 pounds at 205 days) and by using artificial insemination from production-tested bulls. For about twenty dollars (he usually has to inseminate a cow twice before fertilization takes place), he can use the services of bulls that would cost several hundred thousand dollars to own outright. He is an avid student of bloodlines, and his cows have ten times the value of an average registered cow. Outside of the cost of learning how to artificially inseminate cows and the cost of his "jug" (a storage thermos that keeps semen frozen), his overhead expense is no more than that of any other competent cattleman in his area. His gross income from fifteen cows has averaged $25,000 over the past four years, years which were not particularly rosy even for the cattle business. Such profits did not happen overnight. He taught school for eight years while he was patiently building the herd. Somtimes his farm payments left him with nothing to live on, and he had to work odd jobs to survive. Recognition in the show ring was slow. He had bet on the growthy, large-framed type of cattle before they became popular, and his ribbons were few and far between for the first couple of years. His customers were his biggest asset, as they spread the word of the heavier calves and fantastic mothering qualities of his cattle. Customers began to bid up the price of his small supplies to a point where it became embarrassing to the judges who had pinned the ribbons on the short, squatty creatures owned by nobility.

This is not an easy game to play. The breeding of superior cattle takes a rare expertise that is not easily acquired. The investment required is not mind-boggling, but it isn't peanuts either. This man has over $40,000 invested in land, cattle, and operating expenses every year. To match his return with a conventional cattle operation, he would have to invest twenty times that amount and be very, very lucky.

Another variation on this type of small-farm cattle enterprise is the artificial breeding of exotic cattle for the 4-H club calf market. A good herd of brood cows can be bred to whatever breeds happen to be popular at the time. Thus, if Simmental cattle are the hot stuff, a supply of half-Simmental calves can be produced. If MRI cattle look good for next year, the breeding program can be adjusted in that direction. Simmental, Limousin, Chianina, Maine-Anjou, Charolais, South Devon, Red Angus, and Marchingana have all experienced periods of intense popularity created by high-pressure advertising campaigns sponsored by the big-time high rollers of the artificial insemination business. Some of the breeds (Simmental, Maine-Anjou, Limousin, Red Angus, and Charolais) have adapted well to American ranching and promise to maintain a steady growth in registration numbers in future years.

The best opportunities for the small-scale operator in exotic club-calf production lie in guessing correctly on what new breeds will become popular. Usually this means literally buying a pig-in-a-poke since, to capitalize on a short supply situation, one cannot wait around to see how the breed performs. People who came to the Chianina party early reaped enormous profits. Those that bought later discovered their product taking considerable water when unfavorable news of poor feed conversion and fence-jumping tendencies began to surface. Europe is apparently dotted with tiny valleys each possessing a unique breed of cattle. Someday the supply may run out, but it won't be soon.

The best way to market the exotic calf is to wean at 205 days, weigh it, and put it on a solid growing ration. The calf should be halterbroke and fitted (shampooed, excess hair trimmed, and so on). Then as the winter club-calf sales begin in November, the calves should be marketed in two or three sales to spread the risk of hitting a sour sale. The docility of an animal is sometimes as much of a selling point as the pedigree. Parents are buying calves for sons and daughters, some of whom are quite young. Knowing that the little monsters are probably going to spend as few hours as possible in preparing the animal for show, they want most of the work already done. Many county-fair auctions pay huge premiums for champion livestock, sometimes $5,000 to $10,000 an animal. This is why people are willing to pay outlandish prices for club calves. Properly marketed, a 500-pound exotic-cross calf should bring from $700 to $900, as opposed to the $350 it would bring at a common auction. Every dollar over $400 can be entered on the profit side of the ledger. Thus a cow herd of twenty, if the operator guesses correctly on the mood of the club-calf market and does a good job training and fitting the calves, and that's a big *if*, should net about $6,000. It ain't exactly diamonds, but it beats losing money.

A cowboy who has developed his skills as an artificial inseminator can usually hire himself out to perform this service for neighborhood cows. The going rate is $10 to $15 per cow, reduced for larger numbers. He may be called in the middle of the night, like a veterinarian, and may get kicked a lot, but the money can come in handy. A lot of people would give their right arms to be artificial inseminators, so if you develop a knack for it and have invested in a jug, it would be foolish to overlook the possibilities of extra cash income.

Hobby Shop Supply

Out there in suburbia the artsy-craftsy folks are weaving, spraying, and glueing objects d'art to beat the band. Hobby shops sell them implements of destruction and the materials on which all this creative genius is vented. Dried weeds (milkweed pods, devil's claw, Russian thistle, and so forth), straw flowers, and dry wild grasses are popular for deceased-flower arrangements. Wheat weaving requires a goodly supply of straw harvested in the green for pliability. Old barnwood, driftwood, and dry corn shucks are in demand for various novelty productions. Many of these products are available to the rural resident free for the taking. Most everyone has a milkweed patch they'd rather not know about, and Russian thistles are not a basic cash crop, in spite of their marked tendencies to spread all over. There's enough weathered barnwood in most farming areas to keep hobbyists busy decoupaging for the next several centuries.

If a business relationship can be set up with a few hobby shops, these items can be sold at a nice figure. There are limits to the milkweed pod market, but there is no reason why a couple of thousand dollars of extra income cannot be generated through the sale of relatively worthless items. Straw flowers may take some cultivation, and there may be some packaging requirements on all these articles, but overall the overhead costs of this operation will be negligible.

Antique Rejuvenation

There is hardly a farm sale goes by the boards but what a few antique buffs show up snuffling about for ancient truffles, and it is a rare American home that does not have Grandfather's spittoon in the corner or some fragile, moss-encrusted stick of furniture belonging to Great-Aunt-Twice-Removed prominently displayed. These items have sentimental value, which means people have gone bonkers over them. Relics collected from various sales usually need prompt resuscitation. This is why furniture surgeons are in demand. The skills needed for this enterprise are rather limited, but the profits are not. The difficult part is in building a clientele. This can be accomplished by following the example of our doctor friends. That is, put everyone on a waiting list even if you have so much free time you've knocked six strokes off your handicap in the last two weeks. Never allow yourself to be unoccupied. If a customer drives up while you are involved in a thumb-twiddling exercise, go hide in the barn until you can work up a harried, distracted appearance. Blather on about all the work you've piled up and how your ulcer has been misbehaving lately and that the customers are driving you crazy. That will convince them that you're the cat's meow in furniture fixing, and they'll spread the word.

Reupholstery is the most demanding facet of this business. The fancier tucks and pleats requisite in the love-seat racket take time to master, but there is a good mark-up on the sale of material (red velvet ain't cheap), and labor charges tend toward the exorbitant. Repeat business is always a possibility, since once a wad has been spent fixing Uncle Rathbone's childhood padded rocking chair, it must be maintained. Have Junior do a magic-marker mural on the prized rocker, and back it will come for a touch-up.

Recaning is another handy talent that has few practitioners despite the simple skills required. A sharp operator may even be able to hire a nieghborhood youngster to perform this task at minimum wage, while charging the equivalent of ten to fifteen dollars an hour for the labor. The recaning aspect of the trade will create interest in the upholstery, refinishing, and renovation services offered.

The chief advantage of this kind of on-farm business, aside from its profitability, is that hours are flexible and farm chores can be sandwiched in between. Once the business is established, the operator has control over how many hours are devoted to it, depending on income requirements and the time demands of other facets of the farming operation.

Scrap and the Things Folks Throw Away

With the acquisition of a winch-equipped trailer and a cutting torch ($1,000–$2,500), most anyone can get into the scrap-metal business. Most farmsteads are littered with worn-out machinery that can be purchased at a reasonable price, cut up, and sold to an iron dealer. Most farm sales have items suitable for no other purpose. The key to success is in knowing the real worth of the metal on the wholesale market. The price of cast iron, copper, and brass may vary five to ten dollars a ton from week to week. Knowledge of current price and good judgment of the total cut-out value of a particular piece of machinery are essential to a rosy profit picture. Private deals between farmer and scraphound offer the best chance at profit because there is only one bidder. Farm auctions usually attract several junk dealers, and the competition may eliminate most of the earnings. No one is going to get rich at the scrap business, but it does present opportunities for the sharp trader to earn a good supplemental income at an occupation that does not require regular hours or steady commitment. If five hundred dollars is needed to get through the month, then a couple of days can be taken to buy some old machinery, cut it up, and deliver it to a buyer. Cast iron has been an excellent investment over the past fifteen years. With the depletion of quality iron ore deposits in the Mesabi Range, and transportation costs raising the price of imported ore every year, cast iron will continue to appreciate in value. Thus, if a pile of cast were assembled over a five-year period while the farming operation was getting started, and sold in the fifth year, profits of 200 to 300 percent could result. It beats most investments by a long shot, and a savings account does not even compute in comparison.

Most rural areas lack the recycling facilities of large cities. Newspaper, aluminum cans, cardboard, and rags have value if taken to the right place. It is impractical for the rural family to take a box of cans fifty miles for the small sum they would receive. Put a recycling center in the neighborhood, and folks will supply an amazing quantity of profitable material. A building suitable for a warehouse is necessary as is some kind of truck or trailer. Once the destination markets and wholesale prices have been established and transportation cost calculated, prices paid for the recyclables can be determined to allow the operator 100 percent net profit. Thus if rags are worth $25 a ton, and transportation costs are $2 a ton, the price offered on the farm should be $11.50 a ton. No material should be accepted unless it meets the specifications of the end buyer. Newspapers should be bound, rags washed and bound, cardboard pressed flat and bundled, and cans flattened and boxed. Church groups and youth organizations are more likely to put on drives for, say, newspapers as a money-making project if there is a ready market in the area. With environmental cleanup and returnable-container legislation all the rage, the recycling industry has a good long-term outlook. For the small farmer it has the advantage of flexible hours and good profit potential without having to leave home very often. As with the scrap iron business, no one will get wealthy recycling cans and newspapers, but people bringing items to the farm may be potential customers for eggs, butter, cream, vegetables, fruit, or other farm produce. I once knew a fellow with a surplus of Shetland ponies that had become virtually worthless because of oversupply. One year he planted several acres of potatoes and sold them to individual customers who dropped by. He sold two thousand bags of potatoes that year at $5 a hundred and fifteen Shetland ponies at $50 apiece, which was fifty times what they were worth. This kind of symbiotic business activity should be sought after to ensure the success of any particular enterprise. Egg production by itself may be a money-losing proposition but, if linked with recycling, will attract more customers and produce profits.

Custom Livestock Processing

Most livestock farmers use home-raised animals for meat but hire the processing done. The cost for a fat steer can run over one hundred dollars at a commercial slaughtering plant. Such plants must meet rigid inspection standards that require substantial capital investment for full compliance. There are no laws prohibiting an individual from processing his own animals, and, if he wants to perform this service for his neighbors without charge, it is his business. Once cash money changes hands, the operation becomes subject to the full range of government regulations. Income can be earned, but it must be in kind. For instance, a neighbor's hog might be slaughtered, the bacon and hams cured, and the balance cut up, wrapped, and quick frozen in return for having a few acres of hay baled. Butchering service can be traded for grain, livestock, or custom-farming jobs with no one being the wiser. I have heard rumors of some farmer-butchers accepting cash money for their services, but knowing the honesty of these fellows, I assume it must surely be idle speculation. Whatever form the payment takes, custom slaughtering can be a profitable sideline. Since the small farmer should be raising his own table meat, the installation of processing facilities on the farm will save him money in the long run on his own requirements. Construction does not have to be fancy to be efficient. Refrigeration units from old semitrailer trucks applied to a well-insulated room or small building makes a low-cost cooling-aging facility. The cutting room should be connected with the cooler and contain an electric meat saw and a grinder. These two items aren't cheap, but they can be purchased at grocery store close-out auctions at a considerable discount. Slaughtering facilities should also be located next to the cooler and can be developed quite cheaply with a little cement work and some homemade holding equipment. A chain saw is necessary to cut hogs and cattle carcasses in half.

A freezer can represent a substantial investment if bought new. Again, auctions of restaurant and grocery store equipment can provide serviceable outfits at a reasonable price.

The curing and smoking of meat is a rare art form. Brine recipes are passed down from generation to generation. The best of these make the commercial varieties taste rather like embalmed paste. To master home curing you must find a teacher, since the art does not lend itself readily to the printed word. A qualified mentor will help the rookie avoid the kind of mistakes that can kill people and impart some of the wisdom only years of experience can provide. Home smokers are cheap to buy or construct. Hickory chips are the most popular flavor inducer, but many kinds of fruit woods can be used to produce a variety of taste sensations.

Home-cured hams and bacon can also be sold directly off the farm in some states. Where regulated by law, the business may have to be an underground sort of affair. Pork sold in this fashion can double profits from the hog operation. Pork sausage, wieners, and lunch meat can be produced on-farm. If the quality is consistent, ways can be found to get the product into the hands of the buyer.

It's hard to go broke taking a profit.

Milton Tupper

This is an inadequate list of possible small-farm diversifications. It is presented to show that there are many alternatives to farming in a conventional manner on a small scale and starving to death in the process. Nobody in the foreseeable future is going to be able to borrow money for land, grow a cash corn crop, and survive. It is my sincere hope that the large, heavily capitalized operator will continue to lose his shirt producing mountainous surpluses of grain, for that will leave many opportunities for the small farmer to use his size to advantage. Five thousand acres of irrigated corn take so much time and money that the poor devil is virtually locked into a type of peonage where his choices are limited to different varieties of seed and types and volumes of fertilizer and chemicals. The small operator is in an excellent position to raise crops that are in demand and to diversify the operation into the kind of retail-marketing venture that cuts dependence on a middleman to a minimum. Unlike the poor wheat farmer, who must depend on the vagaries of the export market, the overburdened national transportation system, and the notoriously fickle smart boys of the USDA to set his prices, the small operator is in a position to move independently of government policies and the national commodity markets. Honey, organic foods, customer-picked fruits and vegetables, and the greenhouse business are not susceptible to a surplus-induced slide in the price of corn.

Small farmers are in a good position to take advantage of new technologies in on-farm energy production. They can afford to spend more time in raising and processing their own food. By lowering their out-of-pocket expenses for food and energy, small operators can take home a smaller gross income and still show a good profit picture. This is a tremendous advantage that needs to be fully exploited for the small farmer to survive in the years ahead. By adding profitable specialty enterprise to a self-sufficient base of food and energy, substantial wealth can be generated from relatively small amounts of investment capital. The days of the undercapitalized, uneducated, simple-minded farmer are over. Future opportunities lie with the crafty, well-read gunslinger who can see profit opportunities and adjust his operation accordingly.

Here are a few of Farmer Jones's rules that you violate at your own risk.

1. Research any planned enterprise thoroughly.
2. Find a reliable market before production begins.
3. Start small, learning as you go. Never bet the farm on an untried venture.
4. Never count on receiving a high price when determining the feasibility of a project.
5. Keep the operation diversified even if a project seems to demand exclusive attention.
6. Borrow money cautiously. Long-term money for the purchase of land is generally a safe bet if the payments do not exceed repayment ability. Short-term borrowing should be exactly that. If you find yourself wanting to borrow over 50 percent of the cost of a project, maybe you should reconsider.

Show me a farmer who doesn't make mistakes, and I'll show you a farmer that doesn't do any business.

B. J. Tupper

Will There Be Any Plowjockeys in Heaven?

Not long ago I stopped by the cafe to find Crazy Billy and Shaky Ed jawing over a cup of coffee. They had Jimbo Wallace squeezed between them at the counter so he couldn't get away. Jimbo is a young man with more brains than money who paid an outrageous price for one of our neighborhood farms a few years back. So far, despite dire predictions to the contrary, he's been making a living farming. It doesn't help that he reads government bulletins all the time, a bad habit that he picked up during his school-teacher career. He's a top candidate for the Permanent Outsider Award. Thirty years from now he'll still be the guy that paid too much for his farm.

I could see that Jimbo was checking his watch. "Leavin' already, Jimbo? It looks like Ed is just gettin' warmed up."

"I've got heifers calving, so I'd better check on 'em. I had to pull two last night."

"Heifers never calve in the daytime anyhow," Ed announced. "Don't you know by now they always let 'er rip at night so nobody's around an' they can die easier?"

"That may be so, but I've got an extension bulletin at home that says an extra few hours a day spent observing first-calf heifers adds 10 percent to your saved-calf ratio."

"Ah, hell, Jimbo, you don't believe those government smart

boys do you? (Ed only believes certain government smart boys.) I think all first-calf heifers ought to be killed an' eaten. Most of 'em are too stupid to claim their calves, an' they're always skittish as hell."

"My buffalo heifers sure never had trouble calving," Billy offered. "The little fellers hit the ground runnin', is what they did. Ran around behind an' started suckin'. Heifer didn't stand a chance."

"Too bad we aren't as smart as you, Billy." Jimbo shot in the low blow like an old pro.

"Yeah, you don't know where I could get hold of some breeding stock do you, Billy?" I asked helpfully.

"Now, boys, I know what yer thinkin' on. Yer sayin' how kin a farmer that don't get his crops in on time an' is always inventin' revolutionary machines know his ass from third base. Truth is, I've taken some time out to study the situation, is what I've done. While Jimbo here was babysittin' a bunch a' dumb heifers, an' Ed was sowin' wild oats in Washington an' forgettin' he had a brain in his head, I've been lookin' into the tomato business, an' it's a gold mine. There's some outfit that buys all you kin raise. Take the seeds out an' sell 'em in little packages is what they do. I've seen the machine that takes them seeds out, an' for a couple hundred bucks I'm gonna whip up one of my own. Then I'll be sellin' my own seeds direct, is what I'll do. Opportunity she's aknockin' ever' day, fellas. A man's got to keep his eyeballs peeled or he'll miss the bus."

Jimbo's eyes glazed over. I said I thought I'd heard this speech before, and Ed allowed as how he was getting sick to his stomach from all the plumb idiot talk he'd been hearing lately.

"You're crazy, Billy," Ed shouted. "If we all started raisin' tomato seed, we'd drown in the goddamn things."

"That's the point, that's the point," Billy said, bouncing on his stool. "You think ever' farmer is naturally gonna do the same thing. Jist 'cause I'm gonna git rich on tomato seeds don't mean ya' have to run out an' flood the market jist to show how dumb ya' are. I hear there's a market for open-pollinated seed corn again. That's somethin' even you guys could handle, wouldn't take special equipment. Look around is all I'm sayin'."

"Open-pollinated seed corn!" Ed was stunned. "That went out before I was born. Are you sayin' somebody would actually pay money for that stuff?"

"Yup," Billy grinned. "An' they's payin' ten, twelve bucks a bushel for 'er, too. Beats yer three bucks all to hell, don't it Ed?"

"Well, I'll be go to hell," Ed mused. "There's got to be somethin' wrong somewhere. If a man could do that, everybody'd raise it."

"There you go again, Ed. You got yer basic lemming mentality, I kin see."

"What the hell is a lemming?" Ed asked suspiciously. Billy was happy to oblige.

"Oh, that's a little rodent over in Norway that eats moss, an' ever' few years when there gits to be too many of the little bastards, they gathers up into a big herd an' jumps off a cliff an' kills theirselves. Real goddamned bright is what they are."

"I don't know about you fellas," Ed said, getting up from the counter, "but I've got better things to do than get insulted by this half-wit all day."

"Hey, Ed, did you happen to catch that new government consumer adviser on television this morning?" I was hoping to see Ed kick some furniture.

"You mean the guy that says us farmers are gettin' rich at the expense of the poor ol' consumer, an' how they ought to cut down on their food an' all 'cause it's bad for 'em to eat so much?"

"You saw him."

"Yeah, an' if the president don't fire that little creep before we get to Washington this winter, I think some of us boys ought to tar an' feather him an' see how he likes it."

"That ain't good enough fer 'im," Billy announced. "You oughta tie parts of 'im to a couple a Steigers an' sorta spread 'im around town. It'd set a good example fer them other bureaucrats they got down there that think like him."

"Do you fellows think any farmers would actually do a number on this guy?" Jimbo asked warily.

"Some of us American Ag boys is gettin' damned sick an' tired of the government types what's tryin' to run our business. If they don't start givin' us some prices we can live with, I'd hate to think what might happen."

"Like what?" I was skeptical.

"First we come on real peaceful."

"Throw 'em off guard," Billy added.

"Then we ask a bunch of them government jerks to a real homestyle barbeque. Rent some goddamned park or other."

"Catch 'em with their mouths full." Billy was excited.

"Then we truss 'em up like a bunch of chickens an' hang 'em upside down from some trees for an hour or so."

"Try an' get their attention?" I asked.

"Yeah, an' when they get to passin' out an' bawlin', we show 'em a hot oil bath we got prepared."

"A real cookout," Billy said. "An' then what?"

"Then we ask 'em real polite about how they feel about 100 percent parity for farmers, an' if they say they like it, we'll get 'em to sign some statements."

"What kind of statements?" Jimbo was curious. Crazy Billy started laughing.

"Show 'em what you've wrote up, Ed." Ed pulled a well-creased paper out of his wallet and flipped it on the counter. Jimbo read it aloud while the rest of us peered over his shoulder.

"I, ————, am signing this statement of my own free will. I pledge to work for 100 percent parity for farm products to the best of my ability. If I don't fulfill this pledge, I understand the upstanding patriotic members of the American Agriculture Movement will release information to the press proving I am a pinko-commie, a full-time agent of the Russian-Farm Bureau-Rockefeller Conspiracy, and a bad person. I apologize for my misguided antifarmer attitudes of the past, although I probably didn't know any better, and I'll put the interests of this nation's most productive citizens ahead of my own sleazy, procommunist, progun-control desires in the future."

Jimbo said it was astounding.

"Ain't that a kill?" Billy wanted to know.

"Yeah," I said, "that's a real piece of literature all right. What if they do sign it, Ed? Once they get away, won't they call the cops and have you thrown in jail? Don't you think the bad publicity would hurt all farmers?"

"Farmers is law-abidin' folk," Billy admonished. "They don't like for people to do mean things like you're talkin' about, Ed, even if it's funny."

Ed was unperturbed. "That's all true, but the fact is them pinko-commies ain't gonna tell nobody nothin'. Once they sign confessions, we got 'em dead to rights. They have us throwed in jail an' we'll be news coast-to-coast an' border-to-border. We'll become the new oppressed minority. We expose the commie element in government, an' people will rally to us. Then we can really kick ass an' take names."

"Yer crazier than I thought you was," Billy said. "How can you guys be an oppressed minority when yer usin' $80,000 tractors an' got enough money to live in Washington, D.C., all winter in them fancy hotels drinkin' rivers of booze ever' night an' drivin' hooker prices through the roof?"

"I never went with no hookers, an' any man says I did is a pinko an' a liar."

"Is that right?" I queried. "I didn't think you had it in you, Ed."

"Shut up! I ain't never tellin' you guys nothin'."

"You're fulla crap anyhow," Billy asserted. "The worst thing ya' could do is git us parity prices. It'd make all the big boys rich an' drive the price of land out of sight. A little fella would make some money for a while, but then the land taxes would skyrocket, is what they'd do. No kid could do like Jimbo here done an' come along an' buy land. After us guys died there wouldn't be nothin' but A-rabs an' eastern dudes ownin' this land."

"Little guys ain't got a chance anyway," Ed said. "Your efficient operator that keeps his place an' equipment up is gonna be around a good long while."

"Billy, do you really want prices to stay where they are?" Jimbo asked.

"I don't know. Ed here cries about the corn price an' how he's goin' broke, then turns around an' buys a new truck an' trades cars."

"A man's got to keep his stuff current or he can't compete." Ed was indignant.

"Compete with what? A bunch of other dumbasses raisin' cash corn an' wheat an' makin' all the machinery companies an' bankers rich? Sure, prices is low. Guys like Ed put 'em there. He figgers he's big enough to buy new stuff all the time an' survive. He ain't worryin' about your kids or his kids. He's jist out fer hisself."

"Why shouldn't I be? Ain't anybody else goin' to look out for me. Them pinkos in Washington sure ain't worryin'."

"They ain't about to worry as long as a bunch of plowjockeys grow more corn an' wheat ever' year than anybody kin use an' keep buyin' machinery an' new cars," Billy said.

"If they don't start worryin' pretty damned soon an' give us some prices, there ain't gonna be any corn."

"Hell, Ed, who ya tryin' to kid? You'd be the first dumb bastard plantin' corn if it was worth ten cents a bushel. Ya got the habit bad as anyone I know. The few birds you ain't killed yet start chirpin' in the spring, an' you'll wax that tractor a coupla times, fire 'er up, an' go plant corn. It ain't yer fault. It's just like heroin, or overeatin', or any other kind of bad habit, is what it is."

"You just keep flappin' your jaw, Billy. Maybe the wind you make will blow some sense in through all the holes in your head. One thing I do know is a fella couldn't sit around listenin' to you an' make no kinda money." Ed left and didn't shut the door too gently either.

"Good job, Billy," I said. "He didn't kick any chairs, but he was close. Still you ought to watch yourself around Ed. He's been extra sour lately."

"Naw, Ed's jist sore 'cause Fred bought a new mobile home the other day an' he ain't got one yet. I guess ol' Ed is about as far from the poorhouse as you kin git an' don't want nobody else to have a chance to git where he is."

"Ed's right about prices being too damned low," Jimbo said. "If we don't get a good price for our calf crop this year, it's going to get awfully tough. The FHA raised its interest rate again, and most of my other expenses have doubled from what they were two years ago."

"Everyone is going to have to cut expenses and find ways to increase income. Have you thought about raising some high-value crops like potatoes or sweet corn?" I asked.

"I've dreamed up several projects that would make me more money. A few acres of potatoes would pay my living expenses for a year and should sell locally since nobody else raises them, but it's like all my other schemes. The FHA won't go along."

"Why the hell not?" Billy demanded. "Potatoes would probably net ya' a thousand bucks an acre, especially if ya' could invent the right machinery to handle them."

"They've got this rule that restricts their lending on farming practices that aren't common to an area. That means they might lend money to a potato farmer in Idaho, but not to me. If I could do it on my own money, I would."

"It sounds like you're going to keep farming like the FHA wants until you go broke. I always thought their cheap interest got damned high-priced by the time you figured what the mickey mouse red tape cost in a year's time. I suppose you've tried the banks around and they said money was tight and that they're all loaned up."

"How'd you know?" Jimbo asked dolefully.

"'Cause there ain't any of us here that ain't been through the same thing as you," Billy volunteered. "Back in '73, if it hadn't been for my auto-repair sideline, I would have gone down the tubes. Another time the wife's old maid aunt chipped in about ten grand. Had to let 'er in on the ground floor of the ginseng business, is what I had to do."

"I wish I had an old maid aunt to put the squeeze on."

"Don't you think you've got to try something different?" I asked.

"I said I did."

"Then you'll either find the money to finance a potato crop, or you'll be teaching school again."

"I'd as soon slash my wrists as go to work for the public again. Maybe I could cut Dad in for half the profits and plant twice the acres. He's got money laying around drawing cheap interest. It'd be a good deal for him."

Billy grinned and slapped Jimbo on the back. "Now yer talkin'. I always knowed ya' was smarter than ya' looked. I got an idea ya' got oodles of rich relation that a man could tap for a money-makin' scam now an' then."

"Billy's right, Jimbo," I said. "You keep working the angles, and you'll get out from under the FHA before you know it. I've got to haul it. Stay out of trouble, you guys."

"Hey, Jones," Billy yelled. "Did I ever tell ya' about the time I raised them chinchillas? No? Oh, Lordy, lost my shirt on that one. See, the company we bought 'em from was supposed to buy back the pelts at a big price. Well, the little bastards wouldn't even breed, is what they wouldn't do. When we finally did git some hides, we wrote the company. We got the letter back, said 'Addressee Unknown,' an' then we. . . ."